COMPREHENSIVE RESEARCH
AND STUDY GUIDE

John
Milton

BLOOM'S
MAJOR
POETS

EDITED AND WITH AN INTRODUCTION
BY HAROLD BLOOM

CURRENTLY AVAILABLE

BLOOM'S MAJOR DRAMATISTS

Anton Chekhov
Henrik Ibsen
Arthur Miller
Eugene O'Neill
Shakespeare's Comedies
Shakespeare's Histories
Shakespeare's Romances
Shakespeare's Tragedies
George Bernard Shaw
Tennessee Williams

BLOOM'S MAJOR NOVELISTS

Jane Austen
The Brontës
Willa Cather
Charles Dickens
William Faulkner
F. Scott Fitzgerald
Nathaniel Hawthorne
Ernest Hemingway
Toni Morrison
John Steinbeck
Mark Twain
Alice Walker

BLOOM'S MAJOR SHORT STORY WRITERS

William Faulkner
F. Scott Fitzgerald
Ernest Hemingway
O. Henry
James Joyce
Herman Melville
Flannery O'Connor
Edgar Allan Poe
J. D. Salinger
John Steinbeck
Mark Twain
Eudora Welty

BLOOM'S MAJOR WORLD POET

Geoffrey Chaucer
Emily Dickinson
John Donne
T. S. Eliot
Robert Frost
Langston Hughes
John Milton
Edgar Allan Poe
Shakespeare's Poem & Sonnets
Alfred, Lord Tenny
Walt Whitman
William Wordswor

BLOOM'S NOTES

The Adventures of Huckleberry Finn
Aeneid
The Age of Innocence
Animal Farm
The Autobiography of Malcolm X
The Awakening
Beloved
Beowulf
Billy Budd, Benito Cereno, & Bartleby the Scrivener
Brave New World
The Catcher in the Rye
Crime and Punishment
The Crucible

Death of a Salesman
A Farewell to Arms
Frankenstein
The Grapes of Wrath
Great Expectations
The Great Gatsby
Gulliver's Travels
Hamlet
Heart of Darkness & The Secret Sharer
Henry IV, Part One
I Know Why the Caged Bird Sings
Iliad
Inferno
Invisible Man
Jane Eyre
Julius Caesar

King Lear
Lord of the Flies
Macbeth
A Midsummer Night's Dream
Moby-Dick
Native Son
Nineteen Eighty-Four
Odyssey
Oedipus Plays
Of Mice and Men
The Old Man and the Sea
Othello
Paradise Lost
A Portrait of the Artist as a Young Man
The Portrait of a Lady

Pride and Prejudic
The Red Badge of Courage
Romeo and Juliet
The Scarlet Letter
Silas Marner
The Sound and the Fury
The Sun Also Rise
A Tale of Two Citie
Tess of the D'Urbervilles
Their Eyes Were Watching God
To Kill a Mocking
Uncle Tom's Cabin
Wuthering Heigh

John Milton

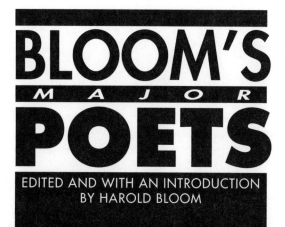

BLOOM'S *MAJOR* POETS

EDITED AND WITH AN INTRODUCTION
BY HAROLD BLOOM

© 1999 by Chelsea House Publishers, a subsidiary of Haights Cross
Communications.

Introduction © 1999 by Harold Bloom

Printed and bound in the United States of America.

3 5 7 9 8 6 4

Library of Congress Cataloging-in-Publication Data

John Milton : comprehensive research and study guide / edited
and with an introduction by Harold Bloom.
    p.   cm. – (Bloom's major poets)
Includes bibliographical references and index.
0-7910-5111-0
1. Milton, John, 1608-1674—Criticism and interpretation—
Handbooks, manuals, etc.   2. Milton, John, 1608–1674
—Examinations—Study guides.
I. Bloom, Harold.   II. Series.
PR3588.J65   1998
821'.4—dc21
98-37751
CIP

Chelsea House Publishers
1974 Sproul Road, Suite 400
Broomall, PA 19008-0914

Contributing Editor: Mirjana Kalezic

Contents

User's Guide

This volume is designed to present biographical, critical, and bibliographical information on the author's best-known or most important poems. Following Harold Bloom's editor's note and introduction are a detailed biography of the author, discussing major life events and important literary accomplishments. A thematic and structural analysis of each poem follows, tracing significant themes, patterns, and motifs in the work.

A selection of critical extracts, derived from previously published material from leading critics, analyzes aspects of each poem. The extracts consist of statements from the author, if available, early reviews of the work, and later evaluations up to the present. A bibliography of the author's writings (including a complete list of all books written, cowritten, edited, and translated), a list of additional books and articles on the author and the work, and an index of themes and ideas in the author's writings conclude the volume.

~

Harold Bloom is Sterling Professor of the Humanities at Yale University and Henry W. and Albert A. Berg Professor of English at the New York University Graduate School. He is the author of over 20 books and the editor of more than 30 anthologies of literary criticism.

Professor Bloom's works include *Shelley's Mythmaking* (1959), *The Visionary Company* (1961), *Blake's Apocalypse* (1963), *Yeats* (1970), *A Map of Misreading* (1975), *Kabbalah and Criticism* (1975), and *Agon: Toward a Theory of Revisionism* (1982). *The Anxiety of Influence* (1973) sets forth Professor Bloom's provocative theory of the literary relationships between the great writers and their predecessors. His most recent books include *The American Religion* (1992), *The Western Canon* (1994), *Omens of Millennium: The Gnosis of Angels, Dreams, and Resurrection* (1996), and *Shakespeare: The Invention of the Human,* 1998.

Professor Bloom earned his Ph.D. from Yale University in 1955 and has served on the Yale faculty since then. He is a 1985 MacArthur Foundation Award recipient and served as the Charles Eliot Norton Professor of Poetry at Harvard University in 1987–88. He is currently the editor of other Chelsea House series in literary criticism, including BLOOM'S NOTES, BLOOM'S MAJOR SHORT STORY WRITERS, MAJOR LITERARY CHARACTERS, MODERN CRITICAL VIEWS, MODERN CRITICAL INTERPRETATIONS, and WOMEN WRITERS OF ENGLISH AND THEIR WORKS.

Editor's Note

My Introduction centers upon *Lycidas* and *Samson Agonistes*, emphasizing their sublime solitude.

The nearly two dozen Critical Views are all very distinguished extracts, so I will comment upon a few high points.

Three remarkable critics—John Crowe Ransom, M.H. Abrams, and Northrop Frye—all comment brilliantly upon *Lycidas*.

L'Allegro and *Il Penseroso*, matched lyric masterpieces, are illuminated by the scholarship of Rosemund Tuve and Louis Martz.

I find particularly useful the remarks on *Samson Agonistes* by F.T. Prince, one of the best English poets of this century.

Introduction

HAROLD BLOOM

John Milton, not only the greatest English poet of the seventeenth century but the most powerful in the language after Shakespeare and Chaucer, is frequently studied these days in the company of Lady Mary Chudleigh and the Duchess of Newcastle. Those worthy women were verse-writers of a certain facility, but their current enshrinement is a vagary of academic fashion. Feminist literary criticism (practised by females and males alike) is an educational growth industry, and for a while our universities and colleges will send forth young men and women who may have read Lady Mary Chudleigh and not John Milton. I myself have encountered graduate students who have not read William Wordsworth, but know the effusions of Felicia Hemans and Mary Tighe. Milton and Wordsworth will return because we need them: they enlarge the mind and the heart.

Milton's *Paradise Lost* is as difficult as it is magnificent; Milton's "minor poems" would be major for everyone else. *Lycidas* and *Samson Agonistes* are both astonishing works; to appreciate and to understand them is an activity wholly appropriate to the compassionate mind and the understanding heart. Both *Lycidas* and *Samson Agonistes* are unique poetic splendors; nothing else in the language authentically resembles them. They are, in many ways, the Alpha and Omega of poetic experience in the English language.

Milton was a great iconoclast in religion and politics, but in literature he was a baroque elaborist of tradition: of Homer and Virgil, Athenian tragedy, the Bible, Tasso and Spenser, and most significantly of Shakespeare. *Lycidas*, the most influential elegy in English, deliberately stations its allusions to Theocritus and Virgil, Petrarch and Spenser, so as to overgo the entire history of pastoral lament. The poem's echoes of *A Midsummer Night's Dream* seem to me involuntary, as though Shakespeare, most dangerous of influences, enters without Milton's consent. Though *Lycidas* ostensibly is Milton's dirge for a college acquaintance, it is as much an elegy for the self as are Shelley's *Adonais* and Whitman's *When Lilacs Last in the Dooryard Bloom'd*. Milton, fearless in all else, expresses the implicit anxiety of being cut short before he can write the immortal epic that became *Paradise Lost*. It would be difficult to find another poem in the language of middle length (two hundred lines or less) that rivals *Lycidas* in imaginative intensity and splendor.

Samson Agonistes is an extraordinary poem, which demands energy of mind and grand resources of emotional strength. Taking his form from Euripides, and his story from the Book of Judges, Milton ruggedly associates his own heroic obduracy and tragic blindness with the Hebrew hero's. Though the poem concludes in "calm of mind all passion spent," we remember it for its shapely turbulence, as when the enchained Samson frightens away the Philistine bully Harapha with the superb line "My heels are fettered, but my fist is free." The fighting spirit of crucial Psalms of David revives in John Milton, who molds Euripidean tragedy into a vast psalm of 1,758 lines, totally imbued with Yahwistic fervor. Milton stood at last for Yahweh alone, which pragmatically meant an absolutely solitary stance, a sect of one. His own tragic hero, the formidable Milton remains the most severe and admonishing emblem that our waning culture affords us as we go on towards millennium. ❀

Biography of John Milton

(1608–1674)

Milton was born on December 9, 1608, in London, eight years before Shakespeare died. His father was a "usurer," someone who made his fortune by arranging loans, handling investments, and buying and selling property. He was a successful businessman who provided his son with an extensive education.

During Milton's student days, he was not a prodigy of learning, though he may seem so to modern eyes, since as a child he learned Greek, Latin, French, Italian, and Hebrew. In addition to attending St. Paul's School, tutors taught him at home, but despite his diligent studies, Milton was behind his age group at school.

St. Paul's School was known for its Christian humanist curriculum devised by Colet and Erasmus. The medieval *trivium* of grammar, logic, and rhetoric was a crucial training for the analysis not only of Greek and Latin texts but also of English poets (Spenser and Sidney for example). This early education gave Milton the foundation he was to build on at Cambridge.

In 1625 Milton was sent to Christ's College at Cambridge. Milton's nickname at Cambridge was "the Lady," apparently because of his delicate features. He was expelled from Cambridge in 1626, probably because of clashes with his tutor. He enjoyed his "exile" at his father's home in London, spending his time reading the books "that are my life," attending comedies and tragedies at the theater, and looking at beautiful girls strolling down the streets. Upon his return to Cambridge, he was placed under a new tutor.

During his Cambridge years, Milton wrote poems in Latin, poems that reveal his inner self more than those he wrote in English. The earliest one he composed in English was in 1628, an elegy on his baby niece, Anne Philips. During a long vacation in 1631, Milton wrote the twin lyrics *L'Allegro* and *Il Penseroso*. The most interesting products of this period were the lines "On Shakespear," which were printed in the Shakespearean Second Folio in 1632.

After taking his Master of Art degree in 1632, Milton retired to his father's house at Hammersmith and his estate at Horton, where he continued his slow but steady self-preparation as a poet. Two remarkable poems that Milton composed either at the end of his Cambridge period or early in his stay at Horton, "On Time" and "At a Solemn Musick," are "small works of art" (Daiches).

He confessed to a friend to whom he sent a sonnet, "How soon hath Time . . . " that "I . . . doe take notice of a certaine belatedness in me." Still, he matured quietly during his six years at Horton: he did a great deal of reading in history, mathematics, and music; he developed interests in civil and religious freedom.

At some point during these years, he wrote *Comus*, a masque (a poem-drama intended to be acted out as an extravagant court entertainment). It was performed in 1634, one of the last English works of its kind. This work is the first occasion when Milton dealt with the conflict between good and evil. *Comus* addressed Milton's social concerns, and it expressed his condemnation of the moral chaos he saw attacking England.

After this, Milton was silent until 1637, when his former fellow-student Edward King was drowned in the Irish sea. This event was crucial to Milton's development as a poet. The shock of seeing a promising youth cut down must have been great. Milton's elegy on King, *Lycidas*, with its superb control of turbulent emotions and its rich variety of pace and tone, is widely considered the greatest short poem in the English language.

In May 1638, Milton set off on a visit to Italy. The trip turned out to be, in Hanford's words, "one of the great *Wanderjahre* of literary history, a moment of contact between cultures comparable with the Italian journeys of Erasmus and of Goethe." Milton, by his own account in "The Second Defense of the People of England" (1654), visited Genoa, Pisa, Siena, Florence, Naples, and Rome. He passed through Bologna, Ferrara, and Venice on his way back to England. He had a particularly good time in Florence, where he spent time among the flourishing literary societies, charming the Italians with his erudition and poetic skill. While in Naples, Milton wrote an epistle, "Mansus," to his host, Giambattista Manso, who had been the patron of Torquoto Tasso and Giambattista Marino, two of the major poets of the Italian Renaissance. Tasso's experiments in epic diction greatly influenced Milton's own writing. During this time, Milton also wrote several epigrams in praise of Leonora Baroni, a famous contemporary singer.

Milton also wrote the pastoral elegy "Epitaphium Damonis" for Charles Diodati, his close friend, who died in August 1638. In it, the sense of personal loss emerges particularly in the question "To whom shall I confide my heart?" After Charles Diodati was gone, Milton had no one with whom he could talk intimately.

He had plans to write a great modern heroic poem, but he was diverted from these plans by his entrance into the political and religious controversies that divided England. For almost twenty years, from 1641 till 1660, he gave himself almost wholly to pamphleteering. The large quantity of Milton's prose writing, which is four times as many volumes as his poetry, is read only by scholars. The most famous pamphlets are: "Of Reformation Touching Church Discipline in England," "The Defense of the People of England," "The Readie and Easie Way to Establish a Free Commonwealth," "The Tenure of Kings and Magistrates," "Eikonoklastes" (the Image-Breaker), and "Doctrine and Discipline of Divorce." For him to put aside his poetic calling must have been extremely hard, but he was sustained by the belief that in his defense of religious liberty he was fulfilling his patriotic aspirations.

In 1642, Milton married Mary Powell, the daughter of an Oxfordshire justice of the peace, who was half his age. (Milton was 33, she was 16.) After only a month together, Mary returned to her parents, leaving Milton in severe emotional shock. In his "Doctrine and Discipline of Divorce," Milton argues that the sole cause admitted for divorce, adultery, may be less valid than incompatibility, and that the forced yoke of a loveless marriage is a crime against humanity. Mary Powell came back to him three years later and gave birth to three daughters and a son who died in infancy. She died in 1652.

Milton's eyesight had been failing for years, and total blindness came in the winter of 1651–52. He claimed that voracious study from the age of 12 had caused the loss of sight. Milton was only 43, and his major poems were still unwritten. He accepted his blindness with dignity and compared himself beautifully "with the wise and ancient bards whose misfortunes the Gods are said to have compensated by superior endowments." He had to reduce his duties as the

Secretary for Foreign Languages to Cromwell's Council of State, a position he had been assigned in 1649, after the execution of Charles I.

These were difficult years for Milton. In 1656, he married Katharine Woodcock, who died in childbirth two years later. On top of this personal tragedy, the political movement for which he had worked so hard came to an end when Charles II was restored to the throne. When the Restoration Government executed some Commonwealth leaders in 1660, Milton's life was in danger. A warrant was issued for his arrest and he went into hiding.

When the Act of Oblivion was passed in August of the same year, most Commonwealth supporters were granted pardon. The story goes that the great poet was spared due to the intervention of another poet-friend, but possibly the new government simply considered Milton harmless.

During his twenty years devoted to public affairs, Milton wrote 17 sonnets and began the composition of *Paradise Lost*. Instead of composing a British epic, as he initially intended, Milton chose the most outstanding event in the world's history—humanity's fall from grace. *Paradise Lost* was published in 1667, followed by *Paradise Regained* which was published together with *Samson Agonistes* in 1671.

The final 16 years of the poet's life were peaceful except for the pains of gout and the misery of his blindness. His emotional tranquillity was disturbed by a falling out with his daughters, who seem to have left him some time in 1669 and not visited him thereafter. He married Elizabeth Minshull in 1663 and lived with her in Chalfont St. Giles in Buckinghamshire.

Milton had a quiet daily routine: he got up at 4 A.M. and had the Hebrew Bible read to him. Reading and dictation filled the mornings. His late poems and epics were composed in his head during the night, and then, when he was ready, as he said, "to be milked," he would dictate the verses either to his paid assistants, his two nephews, or friends and disciples. He walked for three hours in the afternoon, and went to bed at 9 P.M., after a pipe and a glass of water. His amusements were music and the many visitors (some of them well known, such as Andrew Marvell and John Dryden) who came to pay a visit to the great poet and "Image-breaker."

Milton died in 1674. ❁

Thematic Analysis of
"L'Allegro" and "Il Penseroso"

Milton's twin poems were printed, undated, in both the 1645 and 1673 editions of the *Poems*. They are commonly now dated as having been written in 1631. Most readers generally agree that in comparison to Milton's other poems, *L'Allegro* and *Il Penseroso* are most accessible for the modern reader. Even Dr. Samuel Johnson, who condemned *Lycidas,* found only cause for praise in these two poems.

L'Allegro

L'Allegro means "the cheerful man." After addressing "loathed Melancholy," "L'Allegro" takes the reader to an idyllic pastoral scene. The poet invites Mirth, together with "the Mountain Nymph, sweet Liberty" to take him to live with them "in unreproved pleasures." The song of the lark is followed by the "lively din" of the domestic cock. The images of domestic agriculture—the Plowman, the Milkmaid, the Mower, and the Shepherd—come one after another.

The poet gives us a non-particularized setting; the pastoral imagery allows the reader to experience nature in its essence. A series of contrasting landscapes flow one after another, from the "barren brest" of mountains to the "meadows trim with Daisies pide," to the chimney smokes of a cottage "where Corydon and Thyrsis met." The scene shifts from the pastoral to the social entertainments of "up land Hamlets." The evening pleasures for the mirthful man are tales of Faery Mab, tournaments, masques, and English comedies.

The first ten lines of *L'Allegro* form the dramatic opening in alternating trimeters and pentameters. The rest of this 152-line poem is written in tetrameter couplets.

Il Penseroso

The companion poem of *L'Allegro* is 24 lines longer. The 176-line poem uses the same non-stanzaic tetrameter form as its twin. The title, *Il Penseroso,* means "the contemplative man," and the poem expresses the joys of the solitary, melancholy man, and his quest for the pleasures of contemplation.

Here, the poet invites the Goddess Melancholy, "a pensive Nun," to come to him, together with Peace and Quiet, and with "the cherub

Contemplation." Philomel, a nightingale, a "sweet Bird that shinn'st the nooise of folly," begins to sing, and with its song Penseroso's activities commence. He takes a nocturnal walk, moving unseen through the woods and meadows, gazes at the wondering Moon, and walks near the seashore. He sleeps through the day and happily studies through the night. Unlike the persona from *L'Allegro*, he enjoys being a solitary reader, rather than a member of a theater audience. He reads ancient volumes of hermetic wisdom, Greek tragedy, or epic poetry. He mentions Chaucer's unfinished *Squire's Tale*, Torquato Tasso, and Edmund Spenser. Whereas *L'Allegro* looks at towers, Penseroso is *in* some lonely tower, isolated from nature in order to pursue knowledge.

Eventually he sees the breaking of the dawn: it is a cloudy day, with blustery showers. When he looks forward in his life he imagines himself living in "the studious Cloysters pale" of a college, encountering his fellow-beings at a church service. If Melancholy can give him these pleasures, he will chose to live with her.

The opening, ten lines of alternating iambic trimeter and pentameter, is one of the parallel structures in both *Il Penseroso* and *L'Allegro*. In *L'Allegro* the figure of Melancholy is rejected; in *Il Penseroso* the figure of Mirth is wittily cast aside. Specific parallels of invocation to a Goddess set the tone in both poems; the pleasures are initiated by the song of a bird: the lark in *L'Allegro* and the nightingale in *Il Penseroso*.

Both poems take pleasure as their value, and both Mirth and Melancholy are just different modes that require differing patterns of decorum. Both poems are imagined as two halves of one whole; they are companion pieces. We cannot make a conclusion that one poem presents a truer vision of happiness than another, or that the poet is closer to one mode than to another. In all likelihood, the poems represent idealized portraits of two different approaches to life; Martz's alternative interpretation, however, is that the progression from *L'Allegro* to *Il Penseroso* should be seen as linear, moving from "youthful hedonism toward philosophic, contemplative mind."

Both poems show an indebtedness to several English poets, especially to the Shakespeare of *A Midsummer Night's Dream*. ❀

Critical Views on
"L'Allegro" and "Il Penseroso"

CLEANTH BROOKS ON LIGHT SYMBOLISM IN *L'ALLEGRO*
AND *IL PENSEROSO*

[Cleanth Brooks (1906–1975) was Gray Professor of
Rhetoric at Yale University from 1947 to 1975. He was the
co-editor, with Robert Penn Warren, of *The Southern
Review,* and collaborated on several textbooks in literature
and criticism.]

But the most important device used to bring the patterns of opposites together—to build up an effect of unity in variety—is the use of
a basic symbolism involving light. The symbolism never becomes
quite explicit, but it is most important, nevertheless, and in the use
of it Milton brings all the oppositions of the poem together, and
orders and unifies them. I have said that Milton never declares his
symbolism explicitly, but he comes very close to it in the preamble of
each poem. Melancholy is born "of . . . blackest midnight"; the fancies of Mirth are like the "gay motes that people the Sun Beams."
This is more than a broad hint; and to have "L'Allegro" begin with a
dawn scene and "Il Penseroso" with an evening scene, emphasizes it.

But "L'Allegro," as we know, is not consistently a daylight poem,
just as "Il Penseroso" is not consistently a night poem. The day, for
both the cheerful man and the pensive man, embraces the whole
round of the twenty-four hours. If both poems are characterized by
a leisurely flowing movement as the spectator in each case drifts
from pleasure to pleasure, and if in both poems he is the detached
spectator—not the participant in the world he wanders through—in
neither of the poems do we get the flaring sunbeam in which the
dust motes swim or the unrelieved blackness of midnight. In both
poems the spectator moves through what are predominantly cool
half-lights. It is as if the half-light were being used in both poems as
a sort of symbol of the aesthetic distance which the cheerful man, no
less than the pensive man, consistently maintains. The full glare of
the sun would then symbolize the actual workaday world over which
neither the "Mountain Nymph, sweet Liberty" nor the "Cherub
Contemplation" presides.

I have said that in this symbolism all the problems of the double poem head up. Let me mention a specific one: the landscape through which the spectator (as cheerful or pensive) moves must seem—even in its variety—cool, inviting, delightful. It must seem subdued to a mood; but more than that, it must present, when seen from every varying vantage-point, an aesthetic object. Yet even in a poem which skirts the *tour de force* as narrowly as this one does, it must seem *real.* It must be a world in which a real sun glares and real people sweat at their work; otherwise, it will seem a reduced world, or even an unreal, paper-thin world. The point is highly important. Milton must not merely, through his selection of materials, rule out the unpleasant or ugly. That is easy enough to do on the mechanical level. His selectivity must operate on a much higher plane: Milton must give the illusion of a real world, and of a full life—the whole round of the day—while at the same time presenting a world which meets at every point L'Allegro's cheer or Il Penseroso's melancholy.

—Cleanth Brooks, "The Light Symbolism in 'L'Allegro—Il Penseroso,'" in *The Well Wrought Urn* (New York: Harcourt Brace Jovanovich, 1975): pp. 59-60.

ROSEMOND TUVE ON MILTON'S IMAGES AND THEMES

[Rosemond Tuve is the author of *Allegorical Imagery: Some Medieval Books and Their Posterity* and *Elizabethan and Meta-physical Imagery.* In this extract, Tuve discusses Milton's use of "generalized" imagery in the poem to convey a sense of realism without placing too much emphasis on scenic details.]

This seems to me the answer to the much-discussed 'generalness' of the images of these two poems—a bad word for a great virtue. They have it because of the nature of the two subjects, and it is in no way at odds with particularity, only with individuality. Perhaps it is this virtue which makes natural another effect, quite as unexpected (except in rhetorical theory, which directs us to both) as this conveying of 'reality' without the 'realism' of portraying single objects. We have a sense that Milton has covered his subject. Turning, our 'eye hath caught new pleasures'—and lo when we have walked through two or three meadows with nothing in them except a daisy here and there, and past the towers in the tufted trees and the cottage, we seem to have known all that the phrase can mean, 'the pleasures of the eye'. In the 'Towred Cities' which break the horizon line before us we approach all those we know or imagine, and hear the 'busie humm' of every festivity enjoyed in any of them; the feasts and revels so few and indistinct (to our senses) yet leave no such gaieties unincluded, just as all the innumerable variations which a lifetime can put into the phrase 'the pleasures of books' are taken care of by Il Penseroso's little seventeenth-century list. One supposes that this sense of completeness is another result of the functioning of images when their subject is a 'general' or universal, and they are in decorous relation to it.

The individualized character of the images is matched in the time-structure of the poems. It seems to be taken for granted by most recent writers on the imagery proper, and is necessary to the main theses of some of these, that Milton's major concern is to portray the full round of a day, the 'pensive man's day' beginning with evening, but both 'days' progressing straightforwardly through time and all but constituting the poems' subjects. This is surely not quite accurate. There are various *days* in *L'Allegro*; one of them lasts all through a Sunshine Holyday, when '*sometimes*' in one of the upland hamlets there is dancing in the chequer'd shade until the live-long day-light fails and the tales begin—and we do not know for sure how much of this revel we join. 'Oft' the speaker listens to the hunt (he does not see, but thinks of, the way a hill still dew-covered looks *hoar*). Thereupon we hear of him '*Som time* walking' on the green hillocks over against where the sun begins his state. Nor can we certainly tell whether we are to imagine as actually attended the pomps and feasts, at court, for they not only are set in cities, but culminate in the dubious appositive, 'Such sights as youthful Poets dream On summer eeves by haunted stream'. Surely, as we should expect from 'admit me . . . to live with thee', we do follow roughly through the most usual unit into which we divide the passage of time as we live it, but not nearly closely enough for this to indicate the significance of each whole poem's images, nor are the first thirty-seven and sixty-two lines, respectively, thus to be set aside as extraneous to their pattern. Actions take place both in August and June; we watch each: Phillis leaves in haste to bind the sheaves, '*Or if* the earlier season', to lead to the haycock in the meadow. The last image—the miraculous imitation of immortal verses so sung that Orpheus who hears them knows why his own music but half regained Eurydice—has no place nor time: 'And ever against eating Cares. Lap me in soft Lydian Aires. . . ' . Where are we? and whence, and when, does the music sound? This is not the joyful man's day. It is Joy. 'And if I give thee honour due, Mirth, admit me of thy cure'.

These pleasures are of course not the 'vain deluding joyes' banished at the commencement of Il Penseroso. Each poem begins with a banishing of the travesty of what is praised in the other, a common rhetorical device, not unrelated to the method of dialectic which is one ancestor of the Prolusions (of course) and of the whole long tradition of débats, conflictus wedded to eclogue, the pastoral 'choice', and the like small kinds. In each case, what is banished is quite real, not the subject of the other poem seen in a different mood, or moral temper. 'Loathed Melancholy', child of death and night, was (and is) the source of a serious mental condition. Serious but not solemn, both banishing-passages have the wit of contrast (with the companion poem, with the personage praised in the remainder of the exordium) and the wit of bringing out the paradoxical but quite true doubleness of that for which we have but one name. For it is a Goddess, sage and holy, of Saintly visage—divinest Melancholy—who is indeed the true subject of all of Il Penseroso, without qualification and without apology. Her nature is very exactly delineated in it, without waste or irrelevance; the leisurely economy of the images is a primary factor in making the poem what Johnson called it, a noble effort of the imagination. Nobility is a just term for its pre-eminent character, if we make room therein for the delicacy and spacious amplitude with which a sensitive mind grasps and presents a great conception, avoiding doctrinaire rigor and awake to the hair-thin variousness with which men conceive ideas. Melancholy is of course not the conception we call by that name. She presents to the imaging faculty, that the understanding and heart cannot but lay hold of it and desire it, a great humanistic ideal.

It would be folly and presumption, and certainly eludes my competence, to dèscribe with neat labels a conception which not only this poem but half a dozen moving expositions illuminate at length with ardor and care. It seems to me preferable to speak of places where those who read this essay may pursue such conceptions, usually places where Milton too had almost certainly taken fire from them. In accordance with what one begins to suspect is a universally applicable rule, an informed and deepened understanding of a poem's whole subject provides, more directly than analysis, a changed response to its images. Although Milton's poem stands to suffer more from the trivializing, than the vital mistaking, of its subject, its power and delicately touched seriousness can be so enriched by readings which go beyond what I can include here, that I shall not attempt to be more than a guidepost, nor present fully the philosophical ideas involved.

—Rosemond Tuve, *Images and Themes in Five Poems by Milton* (Cambridge: Harvard University Press, 1957): pp. 22–25.

J. B. LEISHMAN ON *L'ALLEGRO* AND *IL PENSEROSO*

[J. B. Leishman was Professor of English Literature at the University of Oxford. His books include *The Metaphysical Poets: Donne, Herbert, Vaughan, Traherne, The Monarch of Wit*, and *The Art of Marvell's Poetry*.]

Nevertheless, although the moods of *L'Allegro* and *Il Penseroso* are less sharply contrasted than in the poems of Fletcher and Strode, although it is only in the rhetorical introductory abjurations and in the personification of Mirth and her companions that anything of the originally crude antithesis appears, and although even Wharton, a great admirer of these poems, agrees with Johnson in finding some mixture of melancholy in Milton's mirth, there still remains a contrast between the moods of the two poems which is both greater and subtler than has commonly been noticed, if not by readers, at any rate by critics. Perhaps I can best indicate the nature of this contrast by remarking that while L'Allegro's pleasures, though far from boisterous, nearly all have some admixture or suggestion of human society and are of the kind which, in some degree, take one, as the saying is, out of oneself, the pleasures described in *Il Penseroso* are more solitary, more introspective, more purely the pleasures of reverie and of solitary contemplation and imagination. L'Allegro, although he scarcely, perhaps, takes any very active share in them, is still fairly continuously aware of the doings of his fellow-men, and reflections of their activities and pleasures largely determine and largely colour his moods. What would his morning walk be without the sound of the huntsman's horn, the whistling ploughman, the singing milkmaid, the scythe-whetting mower, and the counting shepherds? Later he approaches the smoking cottage chimney of Thyrsis and Corydon and closes his round of day-time pleasures among country-dancers and story-tellers. His evening pleasures are essentially sociable: tournaments, masques, and comedies. And even when he is alone he looks around him with delighted attention and is taken out of himself by what he sees: nibbling sheep, labouring clouds, daisy-pied meadows, brooks and rivers, romantically embowered towers. The pleasures of Il Penseroso are much more brooding and solitary. Indeed, only once is there any suggestion of human society, when, at the very end of the poem, he hears organ and choir in some cathedral or college chapel. He begins his night (for apparently he does a good part of his sleeping by day), with a stroll in some lonely wood, listening to the nightingale, gazing and the wandering moon, hearing the distant curfew—sights and sounds more likely to prolong than to interrupt his reverie. He then sits alone by the glowing embers of his hearth and ascends to his lonely tower, where he reads Plato, Greek tragedies (L'Allegro did not read, but visited, comedies) and various romantic poems. When day comes he again repairs to his wood to rest and dream by a brookside, and then, after pacing the studious cloister, first encounters his fellow-beings at divine service.

During the seventeenth century the word melancholy had many different senses and shades of meaning. The noun, in what may be called its strict or proper sense, denoted that dark and dangerous mental disease of melancholia, produced partly by physical causes, such as lack of exercise or ill-regulated died, and partly by indulgence in certain mental habits, which Burton describes and for which he suggests remedies in his famous book.

—J. B. Leishman, *Milton's Minor Poems* (London: Hutchinson, 1969): pp. 129–30.

LOUIS MARTZ ON *L'ALLEGRO* AND *IL PENSEROSO*

[Louis Martz was Professor of English and American Literature at Yale University. He published two books on English religious literature of the 17th century: *The Poetry of Meditation* (1954) and *Paradise Within: Studies in Vaughan, Traherne, and Milton* (1964). His book on Milton's poetry, *Milton: Poet of Exile*, was published in 1980.]

Similarly, it is helpful to read *L'Allegro* and *Il Penseroso* in the context of Milton's chosen arrangement; for these two poems come at the end of a group that might best be described as Jonsonian: poems in the mode of the "terse" couplet characteristic of Jonson and his Sons. First, the "witty" *Epitaph on the Marchioness of Winchester;* next, that perfect distillation of the Elizabethan madrigal, the *Song On May morning;* then the rather labored epigram on Shakespeare, dated 1630, and marked as early by the archaic "Star-ypointing"; and then the two jocular epitaphs for the University Carrier. Out of these experiments arise the two great companion poems, or twin poems, or the double poem, as we have come to call them. Reading these two poems in their original context may guide us toward a slight modification or qualification of these descriptive phrases. They are companion poems, certainly, but they are not of equal strength and stature. Their relation is rather that of Younger Brother to Elder Brother. The parallels between them, so familiar to everyone, should not lead us to read the poems in parallel, as though they were two sides of a coin, or two sides of an academic debate. For the poems develop a linear, sequential effect, moving from youthful hedonism toward the philosophic, contemplative mind.

It has often been noted that *L'Allegro* is looser in its handling of versification and syntax than *Il Penseroso*. According to Sprott, for example, the basic iambic tetrameter is varied with trochaic lines thirty-two percent of the time in *L'Allegro*, but only sixteen percent of the time in *Il Penseroso*. Hence the subtle effect of "uncertainty" that Weismiller finds in reading the rhythms is much greater in *L'Allegro* than in *Il Penseroso*. As for syntax, its occasional looseness in *L'Allegro* may be indicated by the sharp debate that has arisen over these lines:

> To hear the Lark begin his flight,
> And singing startle the dull night,
> From his watch-towre in the skies,
> Till the dappled dawn doth rise;

> Then to com in spight of sorrow,
> And at my window bid good morrow,
> Through the Sweet-Briar, or the Vine,
> Or the twisted Eglantine. [41–48]

Is it the lark or is it L'Allegro who comes to the window to greet the speaker in his bed? At first "to com" may seem to be in parallel with "to hear". Yet consideration of the context indicates that this cannot be so, for the lines immediately following, and all the rest of the poem, present L'Allegro as the receiver of impressions from without—"list'ning," "walking," measuring the landscape with his eye, hearing tales about the "lubbar Fend," and so on. No, "to com" is rather in rough parallel with "begin." It is the lark who greets L'Allegro with his song, just as in the next lines "the Cock with lively din,/Scatters the rear of darknes thin."

A greater freedom of syntax occurs in the speaker's memory of the tales about the goblin:

> She was pincht, and pull'd she sed,
> And he by Friars Lanthorn led
> Tells how the drudging *Goblin* swet,
> To ern his Cream-bowle duly set ... [103-06]

In the edition of 1673 the second line is altered to read "And by the Friars Lanthorn led"—but this change does not affect the colloquial looseness of the phrasing.

Such syntactical looseness is hardly a defect in the poem, any more than the striking variations in meter: these are all part of a poem designed with "wanton heed, and giddy cunning," the poem of "fancies child," warbling "his native Wood-notes wilde," a poem that moves with "light fantastick toe" to celebrate "The Mountain Nymph, sweet Liberty." Freedom of movement, without concentration of mind, is implicit in those floating participles: "list'ning" (53) and "walking: (57), which relate to the wish of the "I" and "me" (34–35) some twenty lines before. Indeed the pronouns "I" and "me" occur only four times in *L'Allegro,* as compared with eleven times in *Il Penseroso.* Instead it is "mine eye"—an "it"—that measures the lawn and sees the towers; and when the "upland Hamlets ... invite," they invite no particular person, but everyman; and later on "Towred Cities please *us.*"

—Louis Martz, *The Poet of Exile: A Study of Milton's Poetry* (New Haven: Yale University Press, 1980): pp. 45–47.

Thematic Analysis of
"Lycidas"

Milton's *Lycidas* was published in a 1638 collection of elegies put together by Edward King's Cambridge friends to commemorate his death in 1637. *Lycidas* is a pastoral elegy; in other words it uses the conventions supplied by an idyllic shepherd's existence to mourn the death of a friend.

The pastoral elegy has its roots in the Hellenistic period of the ancient world (third and second centuries before Christ). The originator of the pastoral was the Greek poet Theocritus, who wrote poems about the lives of Sicilian shepherds. ("Pastor" is Latin for "shepherd.") Virgil later wrote his Latin *Eclogues,* and established the model for the pastoral, which expresses nostalgia for the simplicity of the life of shepherds in an idealized countryside setting. Other pastorals that preceded *Lycidas* included Edmund Spenser's *Shepherd's Calenda*r (1579), which represents the traditional pastoral in the Renaissance; the pastoral lyric of Christopher Marlowe "Come live with me and be my love"; and Shakespeare's *As You Like It*, which is based on the pastoral romance.

The poem *Lycidas* is almost universally esteemed, despite Dr. Johnson's denunciation of its diction, "uncertain rhymes," and its pastoral form, which he calls "disgusting." In the poem, Milton applies the pastoral convention: the speaker, the shepherd, talks of King as the lost shepherd Lycidas.

The poem opens by addressing the laurels and myrtles, symbols of poetic fame. The poet wants to pluck the berries before they are ripe, which means that the poet is reluctant to write verse before he reaches poetic maturity. He invokes the muses, hoping that his own death will not go unlamented. Then the poet describes his and Lycidas' life together at Cambridge and the heavy loss that nature suffers because of Lycidas' untimely death.

But the first section of the elegy shows that nature is indifferent to human loss. The lament of "universal nature" includes the Orpheus myth, which is very important for Milton's poetry. Orpheus' murder by worshipers of Bacchus is associated with chaos and irrationality. His power to conquer hostile forces makes him a classical analogue of Christ, whose descent into Hell is parallel to Orpheus' descent to the underworld. Orpheus' head and harp floated to the isle of Lesbos and gave the islanders his gift of song. This part of the myth foreshadows the death of Christ that brought eternal life.

In the poem, Milton makes use of the pastoral's allegory, as well as the occasion of his friend's death, to express his ideas about the meaning of existence. *Lycidas* is thought to have three climaxes, where answers are supplied to three dilemmas regarding life's significance.

The first problem the poet faces is found in his lamenting the futility of human efforts: What is the use of poetry in the face of death? What if I die before my poetic skills mature? He then hears the voice of Phoebus (Apollo), the sun-god, who tells him that fame is immortal. The speaker returns to the pastoral world (ll. 89–131). Water imagery, borrowed from the myth of Alpheus, the river-god, who pursued Arethusa, links this section with the earlier references to the myth of Orpheus and to the sea in which King drowned.

The second dilemma has to do with a spiritual shepherd who betrays his flock. The poet proceeds from the river Cam (Cambridge) to the biblical lake Galilee, where St. Peter answers this dilemma by reminding readers of Christ, the good Shepherd who took care of his sheep, even died for them in order that they might be born again. Here we have a link between pagan and Christian pastorals. Peter's speech offers assurance of the Christian consolation.

Next, the poet hastily goes back to the pastoral and lists the flowers that are tributes to Lycidas; Lycidas cannot have a proper funeral because his body lies beneath the sea. The speaker feels that nature does not really weep for Lycidas (King), and then he invokes a Christian angel: "Look homeward, Angel now, and melt with ruth:/And, O ye Dolphins, waft, the hapless youth" (l. 163).

As he approaches the poem's conclusion, the third dilemma regarding life's meaning is answered when the poem affirms that "Lycidas your sorrow is not dead" (l. 166). The Christian consolation (ll. 164–185) provides the only answer to the question of death: like the sun that sinks only to rise again, human life is renewed in "the blest kingdoms," where tears are forever wiped away (ll. 168–181).

Now, the poet expresses readiness to go on with his poetic career. He faces a new day with "fresh woods, and pastures new."

The verse of *Lycidas* owes much to Milton's study of Italian poetry. The 193-line poem is divided into verse paragraphs of irregular length, ranging from eight to 33 lines long. The poem is written in iambic pentameter, with changing rhyme schemes. ❀

Critical Views on
"Lycidas"

JOHN CROWE RANSOM ON *LYCIDAS* AS A "NEARLY ANONYMOUS" POEM

[John Crowe Ransom (1888–1974) was a critic and poet, and editor of *The Kenyon Review*. His volumes of poetry include *Chills and Fever* and *Grace After Meat;* his critical works include *The New Criticism* and *The World's Body.*]

[*Lycidas*] was published in 1638, in the darkness preceding our incomparable modernity. Its origins were about as unlikely as they could be, for it was only one of the exhibits in a memorial garland, a common academic sort of volume. It appeared there without a title and signed only by a pair of initials, though now we know it both by a name and by an author. Often we choose to think of it as the work of a famous poet, which it was not; done by an apprentice of nearly thirty, who was still purifying his taste upon an astonishingly arduous diet of literary exercises; the fame which was to shine backwards upon this poem, and to be not very different from the fame which he steadily intended, being as distant as it was great. Unfortunately it is one of the poems which we think we know best. Upon it is imposed the weight of many perfect glosses, respecting its occasion, literary sources, classical and contemporary allusions, exhausting us certainly and exhausting, for a good many persons, the poem. But I am bound to consider that any triteness which comes to mind with mention of the poem is a property of our own registration, and does not affect its freshness, which is perennial. The poem is young, brilliant, insubordinate. In it is an artist who wrestles with an almost insuperable problem, and is kinsman to some tortured modern artists. It has something in common with, for example, *The Waste Land.* In short, the poem is *Lycidas.*

A symbol is a great convenience in discussion, and therefore I will find one in the half-way anonymity of the poem; symbolic of the poet's admirable understanding of his art, and symbolic of the tradition that governed the art on the whole in one of its flourishing periods. Anonymity, of some real if not literal sort, is a condition of poetry. A good poem, even if it is signed with a full and well-known name, intends as a work of art to lose the identity of the author; that is, it means to represent him not actualized, like an eyewitness testifying in court and held strictly by zealous counsel to the point at issue, but freed from his juridical or prose self and taking an ideal or fictitious personality; otherwise his evidence amounts the less to poetry. Poets may go to universities and, if they take to education, increase greatly the stock of ideal selves into which they may pass for the purpose of being poetical. If on the other hand they insist too narrowly on their own identity and their own story, inspired by a simple but mistaken theory of art, they find their little poetic fountains drying up within them. Milton set out to write a poem mourning a friend and poet who had died; in order to do it he became a Greek shepherd mourning another one. It was not that authority attached particularly to the discourse of a Greek shepherd; the Greek shepherd in his own person would have been hopeless; but Milton as a Greek shepherd was delivered from being Milton the scrivener's son, the Master of Arts from Cambridge, the handsome and finicky young man, and that was the point. In proceeding to his Master's degree he had made studies which gave him dramatic insight into many parts foreign to his own personal experience; which was precisely the technical resource he had required the moment he determined to be a poet. Such a training was almost the regular and unremarked procedure with the poets of his time. Today young men and women, as noble as Milton, those in university circles as much as those out of them, try to become poets on another plan, and with rather less success. They write their autobiographies, following perhaps the example of Wordsworth, which on the whole may have been unfortunate for the prosperity of the art; or they write some of their intenser experiences, their loves, pities, griefs, and religious ecstasies; but too literally, faithfully, piously, ingenuously. They seem to want to do without wit and playfulness, dramatic sense, detachment, and it cuts them off from the practice of an art.

Briefly, it was Milton's intention to be always anonymous as a poet, rarely as a writer of prose. The poet must suppress the man, or the man would suppress the poet. What he wanted to say for himself, or for his principles, became eligible for poetry only when it became what the poet, the dramatis persona so to speak, might want to say for himself. The poet could not be directed to express faithfully and pointedly the man; nor was it for the sake of "expression" that the man abdicated in favor of the poet.

Strictly speaking, this may be a half-truth. But if we regard with a reformer's eye the decay, in our time, of poetry, it becomes almost the whole truth we are called to utter. I do not mind putting it flatly; nor drawing the conclusion that poetry appeared to the apprentice Milton, before it could appear anything else, and before it could come into proper existence at all, as a sort of exercise, very difficult, and at first sight rather beside the point. It was of course an exercise in pure linguistic technique, or metrics; it was also an exercise in the technique of what our critics of fiction refer to as "point of view." And probably we shall never find a better locus than *Lycidas* for exhibiting at once the poet and the man, the technique and the personal interest, bound up tightly and contending all but equally; the strain of contraries, the not quite resolvable dualism, that is art.

For we must begin with a remark quite unsuitable for those moderns to whom "expression" seems the essential quality of poetry. *Lycidas* is a literary exercise; and so is almost any other poem earlier than the eighteenth century; the craftsmanship, the formal quality which is written on it, is meant to have high visibility. Take elegy, for example. According to the gentle and extremely masculine tradition which once governed these matters, performance is not rated by the rending of garments, heartbreak, verisimilitude of desolation. After all, an artist is standing before the public, and bears the character of a qualified spokesman, and a male. Let him somewhat loudly sweep the strings, even the tender human ones, but not without being almost military and superficial in his restraint; like the pomp at the funeral of the king, whom everybody mourns publicly and nobody privately. Milton made a great point of observing the proprieties of verse. He had told Diodati, as plainly as Latin elegiacs allowed, that "expression" was not one of the satisfactions which they permitted to the poet: "You want to know in verse how much I love and cherish you; believe me that you will scarcely discover this in verse, for love like ours is not contained within cold measures, it does not come to hobbled feet." As for memorial verse, he had already written, in English or Latin, for the University beadle, the University carrier, the Vice-Chancellor, his niece the Fair Infant Dying of a Cough, the Marchioness of Winchester, the Bishop of Winchester, the Bishop of Ely; he was yet to write for his Diodati, and for Mrs. Katharine Thomason. All these poems are exercises, and some are very playful indeed. There is no great raw grief apparent ever, and sometimes, very likely, no great grief. For Lycidas he mourns with a very technical piety.

—John Crowe Ransom, "A Poem Nearly Anonymous," in *The World's Body* (New York: Charles Scribners' Sons, 1938): pp. 64–67.

WAYNE SHUMAKER ON THE AFFECTIVE STRUCTURE OF *LYCIDAS*

[Wayne Shumaker is Professor of English at the University of California, Berkeley.]

Against this background the catalogue of flowers takes on strong emotional meanings. It resumes and develops an established theme, which, however, is now partly inverted. Although the emotional connotations set up earlier are not exactly denied, they are subdued to provide a poignant contrast to the ease the poet has announced himself to be seeking. The primrose, we are reminded, dies forsaken; the cowslips hang their pensive heads; the daffodils fill their cups with tears. The floral offerings are in fact meant to include "every flower that sad embroidery wears." On the other hand, the coloring is no longer somber. The myrtles addressed in line 2 were *brown*, and throughout the first two of the three movements the visual imagery has been prevailingly dull. The whiteness of the thorn which blows in early spring and the redness of the sanguine flower have only deepened the general murkiness by contrast. Now, suddenly, we are asked to imagine bells and flowerets *of a thousand hues*. Certain colors are specified—the *purple* of enameled eyes, the *green* of the turf, the *paleness* of the jasmine, the *whiteness* of the pink, the *jet* of the pansy, the glowing *violet*—and others are evoked by the names of flowers like the daffodil, which can hardly be visualized in more than one way. The result is that the grief, while remaining grief, is lifted and brightened. For the moment it is made tolerable by association with beautiful objects. At the same time the reader feels relief of another kind. Up to the present he has been under a constraint to imagine nature in only one of its moods; he has been forced, as it were, to consent to a perversion of what he knows to be the full truth. His conscious mind, which is aware of Milton's elegiac purpose, has assented to the fiction that a human death has lessened the objective beauty of woods and fields. But there is a part of his mind which is not controlled by his will, and this part has perhaps been, hardly perceptibly, uncomfortable, like the part of a father's mind which feels guilty about the answers he has given to his child's questions about the wind and the moon. The injustice is now partly rectified. In the catalogue of flowers Milton says not only, "There is brilliance as well as dullness in nature," but also, more indirectly, "The flowers named here are those poetically associated with sadness. I have made a selection to suit my elegiac theme." He is not, then, unhinged by his grief. He does not really distort. The largeness of his mind permits him to acknowledge a partiality in his descriptions; and his reward is the conquest of a tiny but not wholly insignificant scruple.

—Wayne Shumaker, "Flowerets and Sounding Seas: A Study in the Affective Structure of *Lycidas*," in *PMLA* 66 (1951): pp. 485–494.

CLEANTH BROOKS AND JOHN EDWARD HARDY ON THE ANALYSIS OF *LYCIDAS*

[Cleanth Brooks (1906–1975) was Gray Professor of Rhetoric at Yale University from 1947 to 1975. He was the co-editor, with Robert Penn Warren, of *The Southern Review,* and collaborated on several textbooks in literature and criticism. John Edward Hardy wrote several books of criticism, including *The Fiction of Walker Percy* and *Images of the Negro in American Literature.*]

[*Lycidas*] can, of course, survive the most rigorous reading. It can be closely read, for it has been closely written. We shall certainly need to take certain conventions into account as we read, but it will become clear that the poem does not lean unduly upon them: rather it reinvigorates and justifies them. The first lines will illustrate Milton's characteristic treatment of the conventions and the general tightness of the structure he employs. Milton's praise for Edward King is that "he knew/Himself to sing, and build the lofty rhyme." Milton's own poem in King's memory is *built* in every sense of the word, and if we are to explore the poem, we must be prepared to become acquainted with its architecture, and an intricate and subtle architecture at that.

The laurel is a symbol of poetic fame. The poet comes to pluck the berries before they are ripe; that is, the poet apologizes for the fact that his own art is immature. The meaning of the conventional symbolism is plain. But Milton is not content to make a conventional *use* of the convention.

> I com to pluck your Berries harsh and crude,
> And with forc'd fingers rude,
> Shatter your leaves before the mellowing year.

Not only are the fingers which pluck the berries "forc'd"; the unripe berries are themselves "forc'd" from the stem. We have here a rich and meaningful ambiguity. And so with the whole passage: the fingers are "rude" not only in their brutal compulsion, but also in their unmannerliness and clumsiness. The poet is unripe, but Lycidas, "dead ere his prime"; Lycidas for whom the berries are to be plucked, was also unripe, untimely dead; and there is therefore a kind of ironic justification in the poet's being compelled to sing thus prematurely.

We can see in the manner in which this idea is expressed yet another kind of unconventionality. The passage looks forward to the development of the pastoral mode in the poem—the plucking of the berries is "appropriate" to the shepherd—but the poet has taken care that it be sufficiently realistic. We have not, in the figure of the shepherd here, merely the often shadowy character of the conventional pastoral. It is, after all, Milton, the self-conscious young poet, speaking. Evidently this is not the first time he has come forward with an immature performance:

> Yet once more, O ye Laurels, and once more
> Ye Myrtles brown, with Ivy never-sear,
> I com . . .

He should know better; but even so,

> Bitter constraint, and sad occasion dear,
> Compels me . . .

The point we are making here is not that the passage is difficult and cannot be understood but that it is rich; that the words are carefully chosen; that the network of connotations is important; that the "poetry" resides in the total structure of meanings. The opening lines, then, give us warning, if we care to heed it, that the various smaller items in the poem are mortised together most cunningly; and they offer the hint that we shall do well to expect, and look forward to, the same kind of careful articulation of the larger elements.

The shepherd imagery, simply as such, hardly calls for any special comment. It is pervasive, and it is important, particularly in helping to provide a basis for the fusion of the Christian-pagan elements: the "pastor" as pagan shepherd and as Christian "pastor." Further consideration of the pastoral machinery may await a discussion of some of the elements that are not ordinarily part of the pastoral convention—elements that we should not be able to predict merely from the assumption that this is a pastoral poem.

One of the most important of these elements—and one of the most startling, once it is seen—is the water imagery. Milton does not forget that King met his death by drowning. He makes much of the sea in this poem, and he makes much of water in general—the tear, the stream, the Galilean lake, etc.

—Cleanth Brooks and John Edward Hardy, eds, *Poems of Mr. John Milton: The 1642 Edition, with Essays in Analysis* (New York: Harcourt, Brace, 1952): pp. 169–70.

ROSEMOND TUVE ON THEME, PATTERN, AND IMAGERY IN *LYCIDAS*

[Rosemond Tuve is the author of *Allegorical Imagery: Some Medieval Books and Their Posterity* and *Elizabethan and Metaphysical Imagery*. In this extract, Tuve discusses the meaning behind the death of King and how Milton uses imagery and pattern to express the pathos of King's death.]

The subject of all this first portion of *Lycidas* is what King's death meant (still means); not "King's death" nor "Milton's fears of death" nor "his poetic aspirations," but the pathos, unnaturalness, disorderliness, and impotence, hidden and revealed, in the fact of all early death. As Milton pursues the subject, it comes closer to the tragedy than the pathos of the destruction of promise, for the poem almost defines this as the nature of human life. The pursuit will not only integrate this theme with all the tragic human questionings discussed in my first pages, but will arrive at them through poignant considerations of the nature of loss, considerations of the obscure reasons why tribute paid to the dead eases grief, of the scheme of nature which includes man—whether inimical to him, indifferent, or loving, and of the relation of humane and natural; and finally will transform the questions into affirmations through a stronger opposing principle than that of death—and when this is stated we perceive it to be at one with that sweetness which has run underneath all the poem like a strong current, flooding these lines and those, now at the end running open and clear. It is a travesty thus to restate crassly what the poem says so delicately and fully, almost entirely through the metaphorical force of its figures. They could not do this were they not pastoral figures.

What is the nature of the loss? Reserve, dignity, and full expression with neither risk of bathos nor slighting of personal intensity of feeling are but the first gifts of metaphor; greater still is its universalizing power. It is the pastoral tradition that allows *Lycidas* to be a lament for the death of Poetry. So stated, this frightens no man. But metaphor does not state it so. Again we see this for what it means when a particular stance of the mind is habitual. I do not refer only to the fact that we expect the theme when we recall Spenser's October and Theocritus 16, though our doing so restores to *Lycidas* a breadth it possesses but lost for a time in some eyes. I mean rather that (for example) we cannot miss the tragedy of what Milton says by looking at the point upside down, when we are told that King was but a poor poet; and that we cannot think the matter is esoteric, or see Milton as a self-conscious poetaster, managing his clashes and planning his ironies yet dismayed lest his own garland also wither. We cannot in fine read images without seeing the full depth and timelessness of the ancient themes they carry, if we have sorrowed for the death of song when music itself dies in the death of Bion its exemplar, known why Apollo left the fields and thorns grew in them when Virgil's Daphnis died, wept that with Adonis all things die (the beauty of Love herself becoming unfruitful), believed that order goes to wrack when the eddying flood washed over the man beloved of the Muses, the first Daphnis. This image has never meant that song stops, poets never sing more, creatures never couple again, meadows never become green—only that they do so in vain. It means that deathless poetry is not deathless, that nothing is. The death of any the humblest exemplar of that "civilization" man has wrested from disorder tells us that Orpheus will die, and order with him; nothing is exempt, not man's dearest hope or highest achievement; the principle of death in the universe has worsted what he thought confirmed his immortality, and nothing can outwit, nothing negate, that dark power. "What could the Muse her self that Orpheus bore?"—not even the mother and source of that which allied him to the creating gods. All alike; down the swift Hebrus. "Persephone," says Love out of whom all things spring, "thou art stronger than I, and every lovely thing must descend to thee."

How, starting from all this, should Milton not go on to consider the mortality of Poetry, and the withering that awaits all its laurels? And when the Protectors themselves are powerless, and the Poets put to a check, and dozens of poems down the centuries point as does life itself to good that dies, and to evil, decay, all death's lieutenants that take over the flock and the fields, how should Milton not go on to the Bad Shepherds and the sheep that rot inwardly? Men could not have seen these as digressions except by not taking seriously the poets Milton read with an intensity that burns through his language. The pastoral images in Lycidas point to men's deepest trusts and despairs; time had got them ready to mean all Milton was able to say.

—Rosemond Tuve, *Images and Themes in Five Poems by Milton* (Cambridge: Harvard University Press, 1957): pp. 73–111.

M. H. ABRAMS ON FIVE TYPES OF *LYCIDAS*

[M. H. Abrams has been a member of the English Department at Cornell University since 1945 and has had a distinguished career as a scholar of 18th- and 19th-century literature, literary criticism, and European Romanticism. He is the author of *The Mirror and the Lamp, Natural Supernaturalism,* and *The Correspondent Breeze.*]

We are all aware by now of a considerable irony: I undertook to resolve the five types of *Lycidas* into one, and instead have added a sixth. But of course, that is all a critic can do. A critique does not give us the poem, but only a description of the poem. Whatever the ontological status of *Lycidas* as an object-in-itself, there are many possible descriptions of *Lycidas*—as many, in fact, as there are diverse critical premises and procedures that can be applied to the text.

In the bewildering proliferation of assumptions and procedures that characterizes the present age, we need a safeguard against confusion, and a safeguard as well against the skeptical temptation to throw all criticism overboard as a waste of time. I would suggest that we regard any critique of a poem as a persuasive description; that is, as an attempt, under the guise of statements of fact, to persuade the reader to look at a poem in a particular way. Thus when a critic says, with assurance, "A poem means *X*," consider him to say: "Try reading it as though it meant *X*." When he says, "*Lycidas* is really about Milton himself," quietly translate: "I recommend that you entertain the hypothesis that *Lycidas* is about Milton, and see how it applies." From this point of view, the best interpretation of *Lycidas*—we can say, if we like to use that philosophical idiom, the reading that approximates most closely to *Lycidas* as an object-in-itself—is the one among the interpretations at present available that provides the best fit to all the parts of the poem in their actual order, emphases and emotional effects, and which is in addition consistent with itself and with what we know of Milton's literary and intellectual inheritance and his characteristic poetic procedures.

The persuasive description of *Lycidas* that I have sketched must be judged by the degree to which it satisfies these criteria of correspondence and coherence. To be sure it has a serious handicap, when measured against the startling discoveries in recent years of what *Lycidas* is really about. It is singularly unexciting to be told at this date that *Lycidas* is really what it seems—a dramatic presentation of a traditional pastoral singer uttering a ritual lament and raising in its course questions about untimely death and God's providence which are resolved by the recognition that God's Kingdom is not of this world. But surely this is the great commonplace in terms of which Milton, as a thoroughly Christian poet, inevitably thought. We cannot expect his innovations, on this crucial issue, to be doctrinal; the novelty (and it is entirely sufficient to make this an immense feat of lyric invention) consists in the way that the pastoral conventions and Christian concepts are newly realized, reconciled, and dramatized in the minute particulars of this unique and splendid poem.

I would not be understood to claim that the alternative readings of *Lycidas* I have described are illegitimate, or their discoveries unrewarding. They freshen our sense of old and familiar poems, and they force readers into novel points of vantage that yield interesting insights, of which some hold good for other critical viewpoints as well. I am as susceptible as most readers to the charm of suddenly being brought to see a solidly dramatic lyric flattened into an ornate texture of thematic images, or to the thrill of the archetypal revelation whereby, as Jane Harrison described it, behind the "bright splendors" of "great things in literature" one sees moving "darker and older shapes." But in our fascination with the ultraviolet and infrared discoveries made possible by modern speculative instruments, we must take care not to overlook the middle of the poetic spectrum. The necessary, though not sufficient, condition for a competent reader of poetry remains what it has always been—a keen eye for the obvious.

—M. H. Abrams, "Five Types of *Lycidas*" in *Milton's* Lycidas: *The Tradition and the Poem*, ed. C. A. Pattrides (New York: Holt, Rinehart and Winston, 1961): pp. 209–11.

NORTHROP FRYE ON LITERATURE AS CONTEXT IN *LYCIDAS*

[Northrop Frye (1912–1989), Canadian educator and literary critic, was the author of *Fearful Symmetry: A Study of William Blake* (1947), which was the erudite study of Blake's visionary symbolism. In *Anatomy of Criticism* he stressed the importance of archetypal symbols in literature. His later works include books on T.S. Eliot (1963), Milton's epics (1965), Shakespearean comedy (1965) and tragedy (1967), and English Romanticism (1968). *The Great Code: The Bible and Literature,* a study of the mythology and structure of the Bible, was published in 1982.]

In the writing of *Lycidas* there are four creative principles of particular importance. To say that there are four does not mean, of course, that they are separable. One is convention, the reshaping of the poetic material which is appropriate to this subject. Another is genre, the choosing of the appropriate form. A third is archetype, the use of appropriate, and therefore recurrently employed, images and symbols. The fourth, for which there is no name, is the fact that the forms of literature are autonomous: that is, they do not exist outside literature. Milton is not writing an obituary: he does not start with Edward King and his life and times, but with the conventions and archetypes that poetry requires for such a theme.

Of the critical principles illustrated by this analysis, one will be no surprise to the present audience. *Lycidas* owes quite as much to Hebrew, Greek, Latin, and Italian traditions as it does to English. Even the diction, of which I have no space to speak, shows strong Italian influence. Milton was of course a learned poet, but there is no poet whose literary influences are entirely confined to his own language. Thus every problem in literary criticism is a problem in comparative literature, or simply of literature itself.

The next principle is that the provisional hypothesis which we must adopt for the study of every poem is that that poem is a unity. If, after careful and repeated testing, we are forced to conclude that it is not a unity, then we must abandon the hypothesis and look for the reasons why it is not. A good deal of bad criticism of *Lycidas* has resulted from not making enough initial effort to understand the unity of the poem. To talk of "digressions" in *Lycidas* is a typical consequence of a mistaken critical method, of backing into the poem the wrong way round. If, instead of starting with the poem, we start with a handful of peripheral facts about the poem, Milton's casual knowledge of King, his ambitions as a poet, his bitterness against the episcopacy, then of course the poem will break down into pieces corresponding precisely to those fragments of knowledge. *Lycidas* illustrates, on a small scale, what has happened on a much bigger scale in, for example, the criticism of Homer. Critics knowing something about the fragmentary nature of heroic lays and ballads approached the *Iliad* and the *Odyssey* with this knowledge in mind, and the poems obediently split up into the pieces that they wished to isolate. Other critics came along and treated the poems as imaginative unities, and today everyone knows that the second group were more convincing.

The same thing happens when our approach to "sources" becomes fragmentary or piecemeal. *Lycidas* is a dense mass of echoes from previous literature, chiefly pastoral literature. Reading through Virgil's Eclogues with *Lycidas* in mind, we can see that Milton had not simply read or studied these poems: he possessed them; they were part of the material he was shaping. The passage about the hungry sheep reminds us of at least three other passages: one in Dante's *Paradiso*, one in the Book of Ezekiel, and one near the beginning of Hesiod's *Theogony*. There are also echoes of Mantuan and Spenser, of the Gospel of John, and it is quite possible that there are even more striking parallels with poems that Milton had not read. In such cases there is not a source at all, no one place that the passage "comes from," or, as we say with such stupefying presumption, that the poet "had in mind." There are only archetypes, or recurring themes of literary expression, which *Lycidas* has recreated, and therefore re-echoed, yet once more.

The next principle is that the important problems of literary criticism lie within the study of literature. We notice that a law of diminishing returns sets in as soon as we move away from the poem itself. If we ask, who is Lycidas? the answer is that he is a member of the same family as Theocritus' Daphnis, Bion's Adonis, the Old Testament's Abel, and so on. The answer goes on building up a wider comprehension of literature and a deeper knowledge of its structural principles and recurring themes. But if we ask, who was Edward King? What was his relation to Milton? How good a poet was he? we find ourselves moving dimly in the intense inane. The same is true of minor points. If we ask, why is the image of the two-handed engine in *Lycidas*? we can give an answer, along the lines suggested above, that illustrates how carefully the poem has been constructed. If we ask, what is the two-handed engine? there are forty-odd answers, none of them completely satisfactory; yet the fact that they are not wholly satisfactory hardly seems to be important.

Another form of the same kind of fallacy is the confusion between personal sincerity and literary sincerity. If we start with the facts that *Lycidas* is highly conventional and that Milton knew King only slightly, we may see in *Lycidas* an "artificial" poem without "real feeling" in it. This red herring, though more common among third-rate romantics, was dragged across the study of *Lycidas* by Samuel Johnson. Johnson knew better, but he happened to feel perverse about this particular poem, and so deliberately raised false issues. It would not have occurred to him, for example, to question the conventional use of Horace in the satires of Pope, or of Juvenal in his own. Personal sincerity has no place in literature, because personal sincerity as such is inarticulate. One may burst into tears at the news of a friend's death, but one can never spontaneously burst into song, however doleful a lay. *Lycidas* is a passionately sincere poem, because Milton was deeply interested in the structure and symbolism of funeral elegies, and had been practising since adolescence on every fresh corpse in sight, from the university beadle to the fair infant dying of a cough.

—Northrop Frye, "Literature as Context: Milton's *Lycidas*," in *Fables of Identity: Studies in Poetic Mythology* (New York: Harcourt, Brace and World, 1963): pp. 44–55. ⓟ

Thematic Analysis of
Sonnet 18

The sonnet was a very popular and demanding form of poetic expression in the English Renaissance. Milton went back to the Italian originals of the form, writing twenty-three Petrarchan sonnets. The octave in Milton's sonnets is ABBA ABBA, but in the sestet he uses diverse rhyme: in sonnets 18 and 23 CD CD CD (taken from his Italian models, Bembo, Tasso, and Della Casa) and in sonnet 19 the normative repeated tercet CDE CDE.

Sonnet 18 suggests that Milton wrote it in the heat of emotion after news of the Waldensian Massacre reached him. The massacre occurred on 24 April 1655; scholars generally agree that Milton wrote his poem no later than May of the same year. The massacre was carried out by the Duke of Savoy's forces against the Protestant sect known as Waldensians or Vaudois, who had settled on the plain of Piedmont.

The sect originated in 12th-century France, and its devotees sought to follow Christ in poverty and simplicity. Its reputed founder was Peter Waldo (or Valdo, or Valdes), a layman from Lyon, France. He wrote *Profession of Faith*, the statement of orthodox beliefs. Waldensians departed from the teaching of the Roman Church; instead, they based their views on simplified biblicism, and they were critical of the contemporary church's abuses. By the end of the 13th century, in some areas persecution almost had eliminated the sect; by the 15th century Waldensians lived mostly in the French and Italian valleys of the Cottian Alps.

As a result of their contact with Reformation theology, Waldensians raised questions concerning the number of sacraments and the relationship between free will and predestination. By further adapting themselves to Genevan forms of worship, they became, in effect, a Swiss Protestant Church. Savoy had come to terms with the Waldensians in 1561, granting them safety within strict territorial limits.

In 1655, however, these peaceful terms were broken. The lethal decree was issued in the name of Duke of Savoy, who justified his action by saying that the Waldensians had violated the territorial limits. The decree ordered the immediate withdrawal of all those who refused to renounce their Protestantism within twenty days. The real purpose, however, behind the Duke's edict was something else: to eradicate the

Waldensians altogether. Troops gathered on 24 April 1655 and attacked the villages of the Vaudois, who, taken by surprise, fled into the mountains. The troops pursued them and slayed whoever fell into their hands.

Protestant Europe was appalled. Cromwell addressed a strong protest to the Duke of Savoy and also asked all Protestant states to join him in a protest against their "brethren" in Piedmont. Milton voices this protest in his sonnet.

Imperative verbs dominate the octava of sonnet 18. The sonnet begins boldly with an address to God: "Avenge O Lord thy slaughter'd Saints"; "Saints" signifies the true believers in Puritan faith, in this case, the Vaudois. The poet demands divine justice.

Line 5 links the first and the second quatrain. It commences with another address to God: "Forget not" and appeals to God to "record their groans," to remember the deaths of Vaudois in the Alpine "fold" (valley).

The sonnet takes a new direction with an enjambment in line 8: "Their moans/The Vales redoubl'd to the Hills, and they/To Heav'n." Tertulian's aphorism "the blood of martyrs is the seed of the Church" may be applied to the interpretation of lines 10 to 13: "Their martyr'd blood and ashes sow/O're all th' Italian fields where still doth sway/The triple Tyrant: that from these may grow/ A hundred-fold," as well as the legend of Cadmus, who slayed the dragon and sowed his teeth in the ground, from which armed men sprang up. In addition, many critics have compared these lines to the parable of the sower from the Gospel according to Matthew (xiii, 3ff), whose seeds fell "into good ground, and brought forth fruit, some an hundredfold." "The triple Tyrant" is a reference to the Pope, whose triple crown symbolizes his power in the realms of earth, heaven, and hell.

As Stoehr tells us in his essay, the emotion of the poet is "heartfelt, but not unbearable." The almost self-assured tone restrains the shock of the massacre; the sonnet's emotion is, as Stoehr says, "public," rather than intimate and personal. Throughout the sonnet, Milton is addressing God, and his tone is confident. As Hyman says, the sonnet demonstrates "Milton's faith in the ultimate triumph of the saints." ❋

Critical Views on
Sonnet 18

TAYLOR STOEHR ON SYNTAX AND POETIC FORM IN
SONNET 18

[Taylor Stoehr is a professor at Cornell University.]

The sonnet 'On the late Massacher in Piemont' combines this same
tone with stronger feeling:

> Avenge O Lord thy slaughter'd Saints, whose bones
> Lie scatter'd on the Alpine mountains cold,
> Ev'n them who kept thy truth so pure of old
> When all our Fathers worship'd Stocks and Stones,
> Forget not: in thy book record their groanes
> Who were thy Sheep and in their antient Fold
> Slayn by the bloody *Piemontese* that roll'd
> Mother with Infant down the Rocks. Their moans
> The Vales redoubl'd to the Hills, and they
> To Heav'n. Their martyr'd blood and ashes sow
> O're all th'*Italian* fields where still doth sway
> The triple Tyrant: that from these may grow
> A hunder'd-fold, who having learnt thy way
> Early may fly the Babylonian wo.

Although unlike either the young intellectual's complaint, with its
careful observance of the verse boundaries, or the blind poet's
lament, with its tense, delayed-action syntax, the passion here is
none the less genuine and moving; it is only freer and more direct.
Cast in the form of three request structures, the sonnet begins
boldly, not with the ambiguity we have seen so often, but with the
main verb itself—'Avenge'. Thus the syntax, although solidly
weighted with dependent clauses, appositive modifications, and the
like, is clear from the very start. Still, as if it could not be clear or
forceful enough, Milton repeats the opening request pattern at the
end of the quatrain 'sentence', an effect linguistically redundant but
poetically deft. The 'Forget not' serves to link the first quatrain, with
its burden of history, to the second request structure, where the
tragedy itself is introduced with a less direct, somewhat chilling
plea—'in thy book record'. Finally, the sestet contains the third

request, here with an object preceding the predicate, thus culminating a movement from the energy of immediate demand ('Avenge', 'Forget not') to the determined pace of earnest prayer ('Their martyr'd blood and ashes sow').

This pattern of demand, plea, and prayer has little of the stately balance and coordination found in the Cromwell octave. Nor is there anything like the headlong rush of the syntax in the octave of the blindness sonnet. True, the intonation groups are not scaled to the Procrustean bed of the pentameter, as in the rigidly controlled 'How soon hath Time the suttle theef of youth . . .' but neither does any very strong enjambment occur. All of the rhymes have at least an open juncture following them, and there are several terminal junctures punctuating the thought and giving it the rise and fall of a determined forward movement, slowing toward the end where a series of non-essential dependent clauses piles up after the main verb. The emotion throughout is heartfelt but not unbearable, that is, not crucial in the poet's character.

The transition to prayer in the sestet is especially interesting. In the 'demand' quatrain the occasion for the poem is given in the 'simultaneous' presentation of the unholy massacre ('slaughter'd') and the pious history of the Vaudois ('Saints'). The interweaving of pronouns ('Ev'n *them; 'thy* truth'; '*thy* book', '*their* groanes'; '*thy* Sheep', '*their* antient Fold') establishes a kind of holy bond, which is violated by '*the* bloody *Piemontese*, marked as outsiders by the impersonality of the definite article. The helplessness of the victims is suggested by the loss of the pronouns in 'Mother with Infant', and something of the violence of the scene comes through the tumbling rhythm, sharply cut off in the middle of line 8:

Mother with Infant \ down the Rocks. # Their moans

This ends the octave and the second request structure. 'Their moans, although firmly tied to the octave by position, sound, and meaning (rhyming to 'their groanes'), begins a new direction of the thought. The movement now is strongly iambic and upward, from 'moans' to 'Vales' to "Hills' to "heav'n'. The upward swing is paralleled by an expansion of subject matter, from the sharply defined description of line 8 to the generalized 'Heav'n' and the metaphorical sowing and harvest in the sestet. Similarly, there is progression in time, from the past of 'roll'd' and 'redoubl'd' through the present of 'sow' and 'doth sway' to the future imbedded in the modal 'may grow' and 'may fly'. With change to a higher, more generalized perspective, expansion through metaphor, and postulation of future time, the aggressiveness of the octave deepens into quiet resolve and earnest appeal. It is not, we may note, a case of the poet curbing his passion by rigidly adhering to the poetic form or by emphasizing the junctures between the elements of his statement. In fact, the semantic burden of the rhyme-words is especially light in the sestet, and the flow of the syntax around the line boundaries is smooth and uninterrupted. The emotion is public, and ends not in restraint, but in ceremony and prayer.

—Taylor Stoehr, "Syntax and Poetic Form in Milton's Sonnets," *English Studies* 45 (1964): 289–301.

LAWRENCE HYMAN ON MILTON'S "ON THE LATE MASSACRE IN PIEDMONT"

[Lawrence Hyman is a professor at Brooklyn College.]

The dominant theme of this sonnet is usually assumed to be sorrow for the victims and anger at the forces who were responsible for the massacre. But it is worth noting that the poem is not addressed to the perpetrators of the massacre, but to God. It is God who must avenge the murdered Piedmontese and record their groans. It is, above all, God who must provide out of "their martyr'd blood and ashes" an even greater victory over the papacy. And God *must* do this, as the imperative verbs in the key positions of the poem emphasize, because it is God who is to blame. If "blame" is too strong a word, one may think of God as responsible; but in any case, we must remember how firmly Milton and the Puritans believed in the direct intervention by God in the affairs of men. If God could bring about, as Milton believed, the victories of Cromwell's armies, why should He not be held responsible when His saints suffered defeat? "Their moans/The Vales redoubled to the Hills, and they/to Heav'n . . ." It is Heaven who must hear the groans of the victims. But these groans also express the anguish of the poet who cannot comprehend why Heaven would allow the slaughter of those "who kept thy truth of old." The poem therefore not only demands but prophesies the one action that can justify God's ways to His faithful:

> Their martyr'd blood and ashes sow
> O'er all th' Italian fields where still doth sway
> The triple Tyrant. . . .

The greater good must be manifested in a visible sign of God's grace. If such a sign was made visible to all of Europe in Cromwell's victories, why should one doubt that a Protestant upsurge would not occur also in Italy? For every martyred Waldensian, the converts to Protestantism will "grow/A hundredfold." And because Milton is quite sure of this ultimate victory, the anger and shock at the massacre are modified by a confident, almost triumphant tone.

This assurance of final victory can also be seen, although less obviously, in the progression of images. The first part of the poem seems to go downward: from "the Alpine mountains cold" the victims are "roll'd down the rocks," to become "blood and ashes." But in this same line (10), their moans have reached "To Heav'n," which out of the same "blood and ashes" will cause to "grow" an ever stronger army of true believers who "Early may fly the Babylonian woe." The final verb "fly" seems to complete the upward movement. If God, for reasons which in this poem at least are not questioned, has seen fit to allow his saints to be hurled down the mountains (and the faith of a true believer to be momentarily stunned), he will also provide an upward movement to restore both the outward victory and, by the same token, the faith of the poet in divine justice.

The confident tone and masculine vigor, which all readers of the poem have felt, are a reflection of the fact that, at this point in his life, Milton was certain that the New Jerusalem would arrive, perhaps in his lifetime. The year of 1655, when this sonnet was written, marks the high point of Milton's political career and of his political hopes. (The *Second Defense* was written in 1654, and Hanford suggests that Milton began to retire from public life shortly after). We all know, of course, how great was his disappointment in 1660, and what the effects of this disappointment were on his great attempt to "justify the ways of God to men." But in this sonnet, perhaps for the last time, the reverses suffered by the good men may shake but do not destroy Milton's faith in the ultimate triumph of the saints.

Interpreted in this way, the final effect of the poem is not a mournful cry for revenge on the part of an English Protestant. It is, instead, a cry for assurance that the inward grace of the true believer will be rewarded by an outward sign of God's favor. The question of Milton's attitude towards the papacy and the Puritan revolution is no longer relevant. We need only participate in the struggle of a man who tests the strength of his convictions against the ways of God. By carefully following the downward and upward movement of the images, and being aware of the grief that is suggested by the assonance, as well as the strength that is part of the rhythm, we are made conscious of those basic emotions that outlast all religious and political controversies.

—Lawrence Hyman, "Milton's 'On the Late Massacre in Piedmont,'" *ELN* 3 (1965): pp. 26–29.

Thematic Analysis of
Sonnet 19

Milton did not name his most famous sonnet himself; rather, Newton christened it in 1752, long after the poet's death. The exact of date of the sonnet is problematic. In the 1673 edition of the Poems, which seems to be in chronological order, it follows sonnet 18, composed in 1655. That would place the writing of Sonnet 19 at some time in June 1655, three years after Milton had lost his sight. Milton alluded to his blindness in this sonnet, and since his blindness is generally assumed to have befallen him in 1652, some scholars (Smart, Tillyard, Hughes) prefer to date the poem to 1652.

Support for the latter view can be found in the controlled, powerful emotion in the opening line: "When I consider how my light is spent. . . . " This may seem a more immediate reply to irreparable blindness than one would expect three years after the event. Undoubtedly, however, throughout the remainder of his life the poet was subject to a sense of helplessness from time to time, despite his ability to accept his lot in life and the compensations he taught himself to value.

With a pun on the word "talent," meaning both a large amount of money as well as a gift or endowment, the speaker of the poem claims his single talent. Critics have been in complete agreement that "one Talent" represents Milton's literary endowment. Milton uses the parable of the talents from the Gospel of Matthew (xxv. 14–30), and identifies himself with the servant who was given least in the parable. We may interpret the position of the speaker as that of a servant before his Master, a servant who has to continue to do his "exact day labour."

After this octave, the sestet introduces the notion of "patience" in which patience asks for something else: "but patience to prevent/That murmur, soon replies, God doth not need/Either man's work or his own gifts, who best/Bear his mild yoak, they serve him best, his State/Is Kingly." Those who bear best the yoke of life, serve their Master and Maker best.

This tone of determined resignation is emphasized in the last lines: "Thousand at his bidding speed/And post o're Land and Ocean without rest:/They also serve who only stand and waite." However, the word "waite" carries two meanings: the first sense according to the Oxford English Dictionary is "to attend or escort, to accompany for the purpose of . . . showing respect," the second is "to wait for" something (a person, event), "to stay in expectation." Here at the end of the poem the poet, having gone through an interior change, has a different view of his affliction: he thrusts aside his self-pity, and envisions himself in the empire of God and angels ("thousands at his bidding speed"). The two meanings of the word "waite" build on each other; thus, patience not only helps Milton accept his blindness as a way to attend to God as his royal servant, but it also gives Milton strength to sustain expectation. ❀

Critical Views on
Sonnet 19

PAUL GOODMAN ON MILTON'S "ON HIS BLINDNESS" AND MOTION OF THOUGHT

[Paul Goodman (1911–1972) was an American novelist, poet, and critic. His best-known novels include *The Empire City* and *Making Do*; his critical essays have been published in the collection *Creator Spirit Come*.]

Milton's "On His Blindness" is a motion of thinking, reflection on a problem, introduced by the formula "When I consider." But the reflection is peculiar and can be understood only if we consider the feeling accompanying it. The relations of the thought and the feeling are given in the rhythm, syntax, and handling of the sonnet form. And we shall see that this particular combination of thought and feeling is probable in the pervasive style. Let us take up these propositions in turn.

The reflection is an argument on justification by works. In the octave (vss. 1–7 2/5) there is a justification of the self before God; this is given in the profusion of first-person pronouns, "I," "my," "my," "me," "my," "my," "I (fondly)." In the sestet a virtue declares God's position in the argument: "God," "His," "His," "Him," "His," "His"; and further the first person is negated in the words "man's," "Who," "they," "thousands," "They," "who." The transition is given in the alienating epithet "*That* murmur" rather than "this" or "my" murmur. The octave is divided to give a subordinate motion of thought: "these being the circumstances, I therefore say"; the sestet breaks in on this reasoning, indeed before the eighth line is complete, and contradicts it.

But look more closely at the sestet; it too is divided (at vs. 11 4/5) into two tercets; what is the motion of thought expressed by this division, introducing an entirely new idea? For the first tercet presents the correct argument with regard to man's justification: "Who best / Bear His mild yoke, they serve Him best." This is the end of the normal argument; what more remains to say? But, no; now *God* is glorified (vss. 12–13). This further reflection, though logically probable from "'God doth not need . . . ' (because He has)," is nevertheless extraneous, and perhaps even impious, in the apparent unity of an argument on justification.

But if we consider the feeling rising through the poem, however, we see at once that the passion in the octave is not merely the appropriate anxiety at not being justified, not being able to play one's role, but even more it is despair at the deprivation and inaction, mounting to almost anger and insolence, in verse 7. The "one talent" of verse 3 is, of course, first the talent of Matt. 25:15–30, that belongs to poverty, incompetence, and timidity to put out; and that talent is "one" in the sense that it is not two or five. But the talent is here also the poetic gift, that is one because it is unique and great, and that is "death to hide" because such a talent feeds on action and fame and otherwise "I" dies.

We are thus not at all in the feeling of a humble reflection on justification. Then, can the feeling be resolved by the correct injunction of Patience, "Bear His mild yoke"? Not at all; for the "I" must be not only justified but *satisfied*. It is this satisfaction that is given by the joyous anthem, "*His* state / Is kingly." *God* is justified, and by identification "I" is satisfied. We may then come to a satisfactory Patience, the confidence of "wait." The feeling of the octave is not resolved until this ending.

This is everywhere the Miltonic theme. In the early sonnet "On His Having Arrived at the Age of Twenty-three," "my late spring no bud or blossom shew'th"; but just wait! for "that same lot however mean or high / Toward which Time leads me"—and he means high.

And in "Cyriack, This Three Years' Day" his blindness is "justified" by "my noble task / Of which all Europe talks from side to side." Or again, "But not the Praise! / Phoebus replied, and touched my trembling ears." Fame is the "last infirmity of noble minds." And, of course, the justification of God to be even more satisfying than Satan's pride is the theme of his epic.

(This is, I say, his conscious theme; and of course it is only a great soul that can identify so explicitly with such a dark and wicked theme. Psychoanalyzing the same theme, we should perhaps begin to ask—taking *Samson* as his most intimate poem—why is it that to have strength means the same thing as to abuse it?)

By analogy with tragic plays, we might call this and similar sonnets "complex," for the thinking suffers a reversal prepared from the beginning, and then there is a catharsis. Further, by analogy with miracles, we could say that the conclusion of the argument on justification is an impasse, for the thought does not do poetic justice to the gratuitous suffering, nor is it a sufficient reward for the talent; but that God is kingly is a reconciliation *ex machina*.

—Paul Goodman, "Lyrical Poems: Speech, Feeling, Motion of Thought," in *The Structure of Literature* (Chicago: University of Chicago Press, 1954): pp. 204–206.

Joseph Pequigney on Milton's Sonnet 19

[Joseph Pequigney is Professor of English at the State University of New York at Stony Brook.]

Sonnet XIX admittedly gains richer reverberations from the reader's awareness that its author has himself experienced blindness, but the poem can profit from a fresh perspective that avoids the established impasses over dating and meaning imposed by autobiographical literalness. Whether Milton was 42, 44, or 46 at the time, he created a protagonist who is somewhat younger and who may or may not mimetically reproduce a trial that the poet sometime or other personally underwent. In any case the verbal and dramatic qualities of the poem become more demonstrable if intrusive biographical inquiry is initially set aside and the central character is regarded, at least provisionally, as fictional.

The sonnet clearly falls into two slightly unequal divisions, with a question raised in the "octave," abbreviated to seven and two-fifths lines, and an answer given in the correspondingly lengthened "sestet." The dependent clauses of the first six lines established the protagonist's condition (that of a blind servant), character (that of a good man), and crisis (a sense of religious duty frustrated by the onset of disabling affliction). His desire to serve God has not diminished but increased, "my Soul more bent" (1.4). The intensification expressed by "more" carries a delicate suggestion of purification by suffering, and serves as preparation and pledge for the speaker's further growth in the sestet. One of Milton's problems is to have the hero indicate his virtue and express his aspirations toward holiness without at the same time appearing self-righteous. The phrase "that one Talent" helps solve the problem. "Talent" signifies both the money, quite a large sum, of the Gospel narrative (Matthew 25: 14–30) and a *gift* or *endowment*. The "one Talent" is highly valued but also humbly regarded, since the protagonist modestly identifies himself with the servant given least in the parable. And he acknowledges a fault: if his soul is now "more bent/To serve," it was less inclined before, when he had the means to serve; he confesses at least procrastination, or at worst the sloth with which the master in the Parable accuses the third servant. But the speaker's fear of the Lord has also a reverential aspect. He is a good if not perfect man, and the issue raised becomes, how is the good man to regard and respond to affliction? The primary issue is not, as Mr. Pyle would have it, an indictment of God, although such an indictment may be somewhat remotely implied. The dread of death and of chiding, of rebuke and punishment, has more the air of despondency than of rebellion. The first-person pronouns "I," "me," and "my" occur eight times in the opening section to place the focus on self-concern. A sense of personal waste, conveyed through such details as "spent," "useless," "death to hide," and "deny'd," dominates the octave, and not a "bitter complaint" against a "monstrously unfair" Deity.

While Christ's Parable of the Talents dominates the imagination and conscience of the speaker, he metaphorically expresses the relationship between himself and God as that of domestic servant to the master of a household, whose dealings, placed on a financial footing, should consist of mutually profitable transactions. Though this vehicle is transcended and repudiated in the sestet, religious faith nevertheless shines through the protagonist's articulation of his anxiety in terms derived from the New Testament. His "Talent" is "useless"—the ability no longer exercisable, the money no longer available for interest-producing investment. "My true account" refers on one level to correct financial reckoning. The phrase "Lodg'd with me" stresses the temporality of the indwelling of the lent talent; the verb "exact," the demand of return payment. That repayment, in the form of "day-labour," is seemingly impossible in his time of darkness, and so he fears a reprimand: "least he returning chide" (l.8). He also fears something worse. In line 3 the talent had been characterized as "death to hide," and so he might not be let off so leniently by his "Maker" who, like the master in the parable, has absolute power of life and death over the servant. The mercantile metaphorical pattern of lines 3–7 is foreshadowed by the phrase "my light is spent" in line 1, wherein "spent" signifies both the "quenching" of vision and the "full expenditure" of a supply of light. With the word "Maker" in line 5 the Gospel parable receives explication and the relationship of speaker to God breaks out of the domestic metaphor.

The sestet opens with the narrative introduction of "patience." The initial letter is not capitalized by Milton, and this intimates that "patience" is not a second character brought upon the stage but a new quality in the protagonist. In seeing things patiently he sees them with new objectivity and wisdom. He is in dialogue with himself, or a graced and divinely illuminated part of his soul answers the complaining query of his previously depressed soul. A set of shifting tonalities marks the discourse of the persona. He reveals the contents of his embittered mind in a seven-line "murmur," this word defining the tone, as drawn-out grumbling in a subdued key. He assumes a neutral narrating voice in lines 8–9, where he assigns parts to himself and to "patience" and announces the latter's intention, "to prevent/That murmur." The initial words, "When I consider how," also belong to this narrative role. He finally adopts a new and modulating tone in the reply he attributes to the personified virtue. The reply begins in an even didactic voice, which builds up, transitionally through "his State / Is Kingly," to the energized and visionary crescendo of lines 12–13; then the pause after "rest," and the calm simplicity of assertion in the final line.

The alteration of the speaker's tone and attitude is reflected in a variety of contrasts between octave and sestet. The relationship between God and creature changes from that of master and servant to that of king and subject, with a corresponding expansion of the imagination from the confines of a manor to the scope of a kingdom or empire. All but two of the first seven lines are end-stopped, which emphasizes the sonnet rhyme scheme; all but the closing two of the last seven lines are run-on, and this tends to obscure the sonnet form, as though that "scanty plot of ground" can no longer contain the vastness of the new conceptions. A shift occurs from self-absorption and self-pity, supported by the frequent use of the first-person pronouns, to an impersonal contemplation of celestial beings, with a complete omission of such pronouns, from egocentric concern to theocentric awareness. Two distinct attitudes are taken toward inaction, regarded earlier as waste, but subsequently as a kind of virtuous response: "patience," "bear his milde yoak," "stand and waite." The fear of divine rebuke and punishment is displaced in the sestet by trust in providential disposition. External darkness is recompensed by interior enlightenment, with the "dark world and wide" of the blind man posited at the beginning, and the inspired vision of the angelic thousands presented at the end.

The theology of "patience" stresses two divine attributes, kingliness and independence: "God doth not need/Either man's work or his own gifts," and the word "work" refers to "day-labour" of line 7, and among the "gifts" is "that one Talent" of line 3. Not to be understood as a chiding, exacting, account-demanding person, He does not engage in those financial transactions that have caused the speaker such disturbance. "Patience" implies something more: if the actions of God cannot be comprehended under the notions of profit and loss, or of need and satisfaction, He escapes and transcends the concepts by which human beings ordinarily explain conduct and so becomes unfathomable to the mind of man. The speech has already provided considerable consolation and has done so by undercutting the premise of the octave and also that of the Parable of the Talents. One is tempted to hold simply that the protagonist at first misapplies the Parable to himself, since he, unlike the "wicked and slothful servant," has not chosen to bury his talent; it is hidden through no fault of his won by his blindness. However, the commercial presuppositions are rejected not on the ground of mistaken application but on the ground of God's sovereign independence, by virtue of which

He never deigns to enter into business transactions with a creature or into the kind of reciprocally beneficial relationship that the business metaphor represents. A rather radical inference is consequently compelled by the text, namely, that with the figurative terms of the octave the corresponding allegorical terms of the Parable are implicitly criticized by "patience" as theologically improper.

The following declaration becomes more characteristic of "patience": "Who best/Bear his milde yoak"—God's yoke, mild to suggest the operation of a merciful providence, and felt as mild because imposed by Him (and apparently an allusion to Matthew 11:30)—"They serve him best" (ll. 10–11). The personified "patience" most obviously justifies its identity at this point by recommending a patient attitude. If the voice stopped here it would clearly counsel stoic endurance, a humble and resigned attitude toward affliction. The generalization carries an implied admonition, to bear without murmur the burdens mysteriously sent, or at least permitted, from on high. "Patience" goes on, though after the next clause, "his State/Is Kingly," a full grammatical break occurs, one of two periods in the text. The angelic analogy stands apart, in a sentence of its own. From the prior context the admonition refers to calamities, such as blindness, to which human creatures are subject, the antecedent of "who" (i.e., *those who* or *whoever*) and "they" being the generic noun "man" in line 10. The twelfth line extends the generalization to cover the celestial "Thousands" as well, since the phrase "at his bidding" is partially equivalent to "his milde yoak," though with the difference that angelic creatures in an unfallen state are not subject to such evils as blindness, pain, or death. The separate sentence and this irrelevance of affliction signal the task being placed upon the reader, that of relating the account of the spirits in lines 12–14 to the human and vulnerable situation of the protagonist.

—Joseph Pequigney, "Milton's Sonnet XIX Reconsidered," *TSLL* 8 (1967): pp. 485–98.

Lyle Kendall on Sonnet 19 and Wither's Emblem III.xlvii

[Lyle Kendall was a professor at the University of Texas, Arlington.]

Seventeenth-century source and analogue hunting is a risky trade, one that I do not ordinarily pursue, though I own to a fondness for citing *PL.* VII.528 when reading Wordsworth with undergraduates. It is therefore with some diffidence that I pass along to Miltonians several lines from the first, and only, edition of George Wither's *Collection of Emblemes*, 1635/4.

> The World hath shamelesse *Boasters*, who pretend,
> In sundry matters, to be skill'd so well,
> That, were they pleased, so their houres to spend,
> They say, they could in many things excell.
> But, though they make their herers to beleeve,
> That, out of *Modestie* their *Gifts* they hide,
> In them wee very plainely may perceive,
> Or *Sloth,* or *Envy, Ignorance,* or *Pride* ....
> If these men say, that they can *Poetize,*
> But, will not; they are false in saying so:
> For, he, whose *Wit* a little that way lies,
> Will *doing* bee, though hee himselfe *undoe.*
> If they, in other *Faculties* are learned,
> And, still, forbeare their *Talents* to imploy;
> The truest *Knowledge,* yet, is undiscerned.
> And, that, they merit not, which they injoy.
> Yea, such as hide the *Gifts* they have received,
> (Or use them not, as well as they are able)
> Are like *fayre Eyes,* of usefull sight bereaved;
> Or, *lighted Candles,* underneath a *Table.* ....
> Their hidden *Vertues,* are apparent *Sloth;*
> And, all their life, is to the publike wrong. ....
>   (Book III, Emblem 47, sig. 2B4r)

Did Milton recall this passage when composing Sonnet XIX, "When I Consider"? There are close correspondences in content, explicit or implied: blindness, inactivity, writing poetry, hiding gifts. And verbal echoes—light(ed), spent(d), world, hide, talent(s), gifts—reinforce the impression of indebtedness.

The possibility is strengthened, not only by Milton-Wither affinity demonstrated in Allan Pritchard and Evert M. Clark studies—particularly the latter's "Milton and Wither," *Studies in Philology*, LVI (1959), 626–646—but by the circumstances attached to *Emblemes* publication. A sumptuous folio in fours (149 leaves) with 206 copperplate engravings, 200 of them "illustrating" the emblems, the volume was entered in the Stationers Register 20 March 1634, licensed at Lambeth Palace 2 July, and printed by Augustine Mathews in seven simultaneous issues for the booksellers Robert Milbourne (2), Henry Taunton (2), Robert Allot, John Grismond, and Richard Royston.

Such an ambitious undertaking—a monument to didacticism—was not likely to escape Milton's studious eye, whatever the quality of its verse, despite his infrequent visits to London at the time.

> —Lyle Kendall, "Sonnet XIX and Wither's Emblem III.xlvii," in *Studies in Philology* 49 (1972): 57.

THOMAS STROUP ON "WHEN I CONSIDER": MILTON'S SONNET 19

[Thomas Stroup is a professor at the University of Kentucky.]

To put it in a somewhat different way, Patience in the sonnet is also a manifestation of Prevenient Grace descending. As in *Paradise Lost* (XI. 1–8) "Prevenient Grace descending had remov'd/The stonie from thir [Adam's and Eve's] hearts, and made new flesh/Regenerate grow instead," so that in the sonnet Prevenient Grace acting through Patience "prevents" the murmur which leads to despair, and removes the stony from the poet's heart. So in *Samson Agonistes* with "some rousing motions," and so in *Paradise Regained*, and "we may claim as much for the Lady in *Comus*."

Now, Patience asks of a man not overt action or manifest deeds accomplished, but endurance and suffering rather. It requires standing, sometimes standing quite alone, far more difficult often than doing. (Standing, standing at attention especially, for even a short time is tiring; for an hour, almost unendurable; whereas, to march, to walk for such a time can be for the same person only exhilarating.) To stand and wait may thus require even more than to post o'er land and ocean without rest. Writing primarily of *Paradise Regained,* Northrop Frye has given best expression to the theme of waiting or standing, rather than acting, as found in Milton. He observes that Milton was often tempted to work impulsively, to chaff at having to wait till the appointed time. "This problem, in itself peculiar to Milton as a poet, was for him also a special case of the general principle that the Christian must learn to will to relax the will, to perform real acts in God's time and not pseudo-acts in his own. In the temptations of Adam and Samson the same theme recurs of an action not so much wrong in itself as wrong at that time, a hasty snatching of a chance before the real time has been fulfilled in itself. Christ is older [in *Paradise Regained*] than Milton was at twenty-three when he wrote the famous sonnet, and Satan is constantly urging him, from the first temptation on, to be his own providence, to release some of his latent energies." What Frye says here is quite as applicable to the sonnet "On His Blindness" as to the poems mentioned. It requires the standing and waiting, for the time is not yet, any more than it was for him at twenty-three or Jesus at thirty. And even if it never comes, he can yet will to relax his will before God's will and be satisfied in his readiness as the true warfaring Christian.

—Thomas Stroup, "'When I Consider': Milton's Sonnet XIX," in *Studies in Philology* 69 (1972): pp. 252–53.

Thematic Analysis of
Sonnet 23

This sonnet describes a dream with a powerful concentration of emotion. Tradition assumes that Milton speaks in the sonnet about his second wife, Katherine Woodcock, who died in February 1658. Some commentators have said, though, that the sonnet speaks of Milton's first wife, Mary Powell. Leo Spitzer proposes that the "late espoused Saint" is an ideal figure like Dante's and Petrarch's *donna angelicata,* whereas Wheeler suggests that Milton portrays his ideal mate, the mate for whom he longed but never found.

"Late espoused Saint" comes into the speaker's dream like Alcestis, the wife of Admetus who gave her life as a ransom for her husband. Hercules, Jove's son, according to Greek myth, wrestles with Thanatos (death) and forces him to give up Alcestis; then Hercules brings her back to her husband. Alcestis is veiled as is Milton's "saint," who "came vested all in white, pure as her mind: her face was vail'd" (lines 8 and 9). In his fancy, the speaker sees only the "love, sweetness, goodness" that shone in her person.

The monosyllabic last line bears all the emotional weight of the poem. As she inclined to embrace him in the dream he "wak'd, she fled, and day brought back (his) night." Waking up fills him with anguish and dismay. ❀

Critical Views on
Sonnet 23

THOMAS WHEELER ON MILTON'S 23RD SONNET

[Thomas Wheeler is a professor at the University of Tennessee.]

I suggest that sonnet XXIII is best interpreted if we remember this facet of Milton's mind. He is writing primarily about loss—the almost insufferable loss of a beloved woman. It seems unlikely that Mary Powell, from whom he sought a divorce, could be the subject of his longing. And if he meant Katherine Woodcock, then he was wrong about "purification in the old Law," a possibility which one ought to keep in mind. But even if Milton did refer to Katherine and did make a mistake in referring to the Mosaic law, the figure presented in the poem is clearly idealized. She

> Came vested all in white, pure as her mind:
>> Her face was vail'd, yet to my fancied sight,
>> Love, sweetness, goodness, in her person shin'd
> So clear, as in no face with more delight.

This is not Katherine Woodcock; it is an ideal in the mind of John Milton. Regardless of whether the poem got its start in an actual dream or not, it represents what every dream represents: the shaping of reality by the mind. It is not Mary Powell or Katherine that Milton longs for; it is that "apt and cheerful conversation of man with woman" that he never found. It is the kind of Paradise depicted in the Garden: Eve, beautiful, womanly, and submissive; Adam whispering to Eve

>> Awake
> My fairest, my espous'd my latest found,
> Heavens last best gift, my ever new delight . . .

and Eve answering

> O Sole in whom my thoughts find all repose,
> My Glorie, my Perfection. . . .

The poignant grief of the sonnet reminds one of Satan's anguish as he beholds the nuptial bliss of Adam and Eve.

> Sight hateful, sight tormenting! thus these two
> Imparadis't in one anothers arms
> The happier *Eden*, shall enjoy thir fill
> Of bliss on bliss while I to Hell am thrust,
> Where neither joy nor love, but fierce desire,
> Among our other torments not the least,
> Still unfulfill'd with pain of longing pines.

Even more to the point is another dream, narrated in *Paradise Lost*, a dream which is obviously fictitious, yet so much like sonnet XXIII that one can hardly believe that Milton wrote without the sonnet in mind. Adam is telling Raphael about the creation of Eve.

> The Rib he formd and fashond with his hands;
> Under his forming hands a Creature grew,
> Manlike, but different sex, so lovly faire
> That what seemd fair in all the World, seemd now
> Mean, or in her summd up, in her containd
> And in her looks, which from that time infus'd
> Sweetness into my heart, unfelt before,
> And into all things from her Aire inspir'd
> The spirit of love and amorous delight.
> She disappeerd, and left me dark, I wak'd
> To find her, or for ever to deplore
> Her loss, and other pleasures all abjure

It is no *donna angelicata* of Dante that Milton dreams of but the very image in his mind of a paradise which, like Adam, he sought but never found.

This interpretation of the sonnet has two distinct advantages. First, it makes unnecessary a controversy which adds nothing to our understanding and appreciation of the sonnet. To any sensitive reader the important fact about the poem is the sense of almost unutterable loneliness and the suffocating isolation of the man whose day is night. It makes no difference who he is talking about. The Mary Powell–Katherine Woodcock argument is, no pun intended, a blind alley.

But one might wish to see in this sonnet something of its author's mind. The interpretation I suggest has this second advantage. It connects this poem with the mind of Milton as we see it in many of his other works and deepens our response to the pathos of Milton's situation for he has nowhere to live but in his mind, and he has not even the remembrance of an ideal marriage, only the ideal itself which he cannot seize in the midst of his darkness. No other poem shows us so poignantly Milton's sense of isolation. Not even *Samson Agonistes* carries the power of this brief lyric, for Samson will know a last moment of triumph but John Milton will live out his life in darkness.

Finally I think we see in sonnet XXIII one other aspect of Milton's mind: his tendency to dramatize himself. The man who, in the *Second Defense*, saw himself surveying "as if from a towering height, the far extended tracts of sea and land and innumerable crowds of spectators betraying in their looks the liveliest interest and sensations most congenial with [his] own," now sees himself alone, lonely, and in the dark. And while it is prudent, as I have said, to assume that Milton's dream was substantially as he described it, the dream is almost too dramatic, too good a subject for a sonnet. Regardless of what has been said about the sonnet "On the Late Massacre in Piemont," it seems to me that sonnet XXIII is the most compellingly powerful of all Milton's lyrics. May it not be that to dramatize his loneliness and sense of loss Milton has improved upon his dream? Has he not in the magnificent compression of the sestet showed himself to be still the poet, the maker, raising his experience above the level of prosaic reality to the regions of charmed song?

—Thomas Wheeler, "Milton's Twenty-Third Sonnet," Studies in Philology 58 (1961): pp. 510–15.

LEO SPITZER ON UNDERSTANDING MILTON IN SONNET 23

[Leo Spitzer taught at John Hopkins University from 1936 until his death in 1960. He enjoyed a reputation as one of the twentieth century's outstanding philologists and linguists. His books include: *Essays in Historical Semantics* (1948), *Linguistics and Literary History* (1948), and *A Method of Interpreting Literature* (1949).]

That the true meaning of the poem "Methought" can be grasped only by a reader who has experienced blindness and that the specific physical sensations of a blind man were of any importance to the poet, is utterly refuted by the two sonnets devoted precisely to his blindness—wherein we find this condition referred to briefly and in the most general terms ("my sight is spent," the world has become "dark"), accessible to any member of the human community, the main emphasis being placed on the *moral* problems involved in this condition. When faced with the sonnet "Methought," then, the "Poor-blind-twice-widowed-Milton-wrote-this-poem-in-a-dreary-apartment-alone-with-his-small-children" school of thought (Masson *et al*) must definitely yield to that of the less sentimental and more factual literary historians concerned with the *dolce stil nuovo* of Dante and Petrarch. Not only is the reader of the sonnet not obliged to speculate about the probable complexities of Milton's empirical life outside of the poem; he is obliged not to so speculate.

It is a quite illegitimate procedure, one most detrimental to any *explication de texte* (although widely current with our academic positivism), to "utilize" indiscriminately "what we know of the poet's biography," because this may destroy the artistic framework carefully devised by the poet: the boundary between art and life which he perhaps may have wished to erect—and which any classical poet would be apt to erect. Professor Boas is disappointed by Shakespeare's "mathematical" generality in his love poems mainly because this poet has succeeded (aided therein by the fruitlessness of all "pedantic' investigations) in keeping us in the dark about the particular persons to whom he addressed his sonnets; Boas is more at home with Milton, who has at least himself half-lifted the veils from his autobiography (his biographers, also, having been successful in uncovering the facts of his life), but not quite happy because the singular experiences of the historical Milton make it difficult for us to know exactly what "he saw and felt when he dreamed of Katherine Woodcock." To me the brusque introduction of the matter-of-fact, opaque name Katherine Woodcock into the transparent and transcendent atmosphere of our poem is as shocking as the whole proposition of making the poem more empirically concrete than it has been conceived. The poem should, in my opinion, be apperceived *half-concretely* as it was intended to be. Such is the tact and discipline required from the reader, who should not indulge in unwarranted psychological or historical curiosity, but should abdicate such inquiry when it is nocive to artistic apperception.

—Leo Spitzer, "Understanding Milton" in *Essays on English and American Literature* (Princeton: Princeton University Press, 1962): pp. 127–29.

Thematic Analysis of
"Samson Agonistes"

The story of Samson is given in the Old Testament, in the Book of Judges, chapters XIII–XVI. As the title of the poem indicates ("agonistes" means "in struggle" or "under trial"), Milton's poem presents only the few hours before Samson's death. The word "agonistes" comes from the Greek term for a wrestler, and it implies that Samson in his final hours is both a spiritual and physical athlete.

The title follows the form of these Greek tragedies: *Prometheus Bound* by Aeschylus and *Oedipus at Colonnus* by Sophocles; it also is similar to the Renaissance followers of the convention, such as Ariosto in the *Orlando Furioso* and Tasso in *Jerusalem Liberated.*

The preface "Of that sort of Dramatic Poem which is called Tragedy" suggests two purposes: to suggest that the ancient Greek tragedy is the only model for this drama and to remind the reader of the spiritual value of tragic drama. As a Puritan, Milton no doubt felt the need to justify his reasons for writing a drama, since Puritans regarded stage plays as a serious moral danger. Finding sufficient spiritual justification for its writing, Milton wrote what was known as a "closet drama," one that was intended not for the actual stage but for private reading.

The biblical Samson must have appealed to Milton—after all, like Milton, Samson experienced an unhappy marriage, and like Milton, he triumphed spiritually over physical blindness. More important, however, from Milton's point of view, was the fact that Samson suffered for the sake of his people's freedom; in the pit of disappear and failure, he experienced God's grace, enabling him to die heroically and triumphantly.

As F. T. Prince has stated, *Samson Agonistes* can be analyzed in a way that corresponds closely to its Greek precedents. The first 114 lines of Samson's soliloquy is a *prologue.* After that follows a *parodos,* 61 lines spoken by the Chorus when it first enters and before it addresses Samson. The first *epeisodion* (ll. 176–292) consists of the dialogue between Samson and the chorus, followed by the choral ode, the first stasimon (ll. 292–325). The second *epeisodion* begins when Samson's father, Manoa, enters (l. 326); the third *epeisodion* is the dialogue between Samson and Dalila (ll. 1009–1061), the fourth, the exchange between Samson and Harapha (ll.1061–1267); the fifth is the visit of a Philistine official, after which Samson departs to the festival of Dagon (ll. 1301–1426). When Manoa comes back, the *exodos* of the play begins (ll. 1441), and continues until the Messenger tells the story of Samson's death. The Chorus is on the stage throughout, and gives comments on each episode in a *stasimon*.

Samson enters, led by a guide who leaves the stage without having spoken. (The Greeks called such characters "silent actors.") In a long soliloquy, Samson tells what gives him the opportunity to rest: the Philistines' feast in honor of Dagon. He describes the torments of mind and miseries of blindness. He contrasts his present state with the promises which had preceded his birth, as one who was chosen by God to do great deeds for his country. However, he lost God's destiny for his life when he revealed to his wife (a Philistine woman) that the source of his strength lay in his hair. For that "telling" he blames only himself, his weakness of will. "What is strength without a double share of wisdom?" he asks himself.

His speech in blank verse becomes a lyrical lament, and when interrupted by the approaching Chorus, goes back to blank verse.

The Chorus first comments on Samson's appearance, and compares it with his former power that "no strength of man, or fiercest wild beast could withstand"(l. 127). The Chorus presents itself to Samson as a group of his friends and neighbors, who come to lament his misfortune, give him advice, and comfort him with the apt words that can calm the troubled mind. Samson welcomes them as true friends, since they didn't leave him to be alone in his misery. Although it's a matter of wonder why Samson married a Philistine woman, Samson repeats that she was not the cause of his suffering. The Chorus also points out that Samson has not succeeded in liberating the Israelites from the Philistines, and Samson replies that the leaders of Israel actually did not support his enterprises. The Chorus asserts God's justice and breaks off to announce the entry of Manoa, Samson's aged father.

When Manoa laments his son's disgrace, Samson once more restates that he is fully responsible for it. From Manoa's speech we find out that he has proposed his son's ransom to the Philistines.

Samson says he would rather endure the punishment. His hopes "are flat," and "the nature within him seems in all her functions weary of herself." Here Milton introduces the ransom to create the dramatic effect of expectation and suspense.

Manoa's visit creates total despair in Samson. Feeling the depth of it, the Chorus muses over God's treatment of his chosen ones. Dalila approaches Samson, and acknowledging her fault, asks Samson for forgiveness. Samson rejects her plea. She speaks of the affection she can offer him, but he refuses; she tempts his senses, but his reaction is ferocious. When she realizes she has no power over him anymore, that the force of her charms is nulled, she tells him she will find compensation in the gratitude of the Philistines, who will treat her as a national heroine. Samson's inflexibility in the face of temptation impresses the Chorus.

Milton puts the encounter of Samson and Dalila in the center of his play. When Samson will not yield to her charms, it represents the turning point in his life. The effect on Samson of Dalila's visit is decisive. He is roused from his lethargy, because of his moral strength to reject her offers; he chooses his misery over the pleasures of her home.

Then comes Harapha, a Philistine. He has come to see the famous Hebrew champion and to check on his strength. If they had met before, he says, Harapha would have surely won. Samson challenges him now, but Harapha doesn't want to undertake the test of strength. The exchange of fierce words brings another change to Samson: He realizes that not only is his strength coming back but also his desire for action. He hints that he may seek revenge.

A Philistine official comes and commands that Samson appear before the Philistine people at Dagon's festival and entertain them with feats of strength. Samson refuses determinedly. The officer issues threats. While Samson is justifying his refusal, a completely new thought strikes him; he changes his mind, informing the Chorus that he will obey the Philistines' command. When the Philistine officer returns, Samson agrees to go with him.

The pace of the action quickens. Manoa returns full of hope for his son's ransom. A conversation with the chorus is interrupted, first by a shout that "tore the sky," and then by a hideous noise that leaves the Chorus and Manoa terrified. An Israelite then arrives and describes the horrid scene he witnessed. "Samson is dead"—that is the worst part of the news—but he died triumphantly. When Samson entered the temple, he tugged and shook the pillars till they fell, bringing down the roof upon the heads of the Philistines and himself.

Manoa's final speech is full of pride for his son's death. The Chorus ends the play with a hymn in praise of Divine Providence:

> Of true experience from this great event
> With peace and consolation hath dismiss'd,
> And calm of mind, all passion spent. ❁

Critical Views on
"Samson Agonistes"

DAVID DAICHES ON *SAMSON AGONISTES*

[David Daiches is Professor of English in the University of Sussex.]

In *Samson Agonistes* Milton finally produced the biblical tragedy which he had long ago prescribed as the kind of literature to be encouraged in a Christian society. The form is that of Greek tragedy, with Sophocles' *Oedipus at Colonnus* and Aeschylus' *Prometheus Bound* serving as models. Milton explains in an introduction that "tragedy, as it was antiently compos'd, hath been ever held the gravest, moralest, and most profitable of all other Poems: therefore said by *Aristotle* to be of power by raising pity and fear, or terror, to purge the mind of those and such like passions, that is to temper and reduce them to just measure with a kind of delight, stirr'd up by reading or seeing those passions well imitated'. He goes on to cite other evidence of the gravity and high seriousness of tragedy, testified to by Cicero, Plutarch, Seneca and others, among them a Father of the Church. His models, he continues, are both the Greeks and the Italians, and 'the measure of verse us'd in the Chorus is of all sorts'. The introduction concludes:

> Of the style and uniformitie, and that commonly call'd the Plot, whether intricate or explicit, which is nothing indeed but such œconomy or disposition of the fable as may stand best with verisimilitude and decorum; they only will best judge who are not unacquainted with *Æschulus, Sophocles,* and *Euripides,* the three Tragic Poets unequall'd yet by any, and the best rule to all who endeavour to write Tragedy. The circumscription of time wherein the whole Drama begins and ends, is according to antient rule, and best example, within the space of 24 hours.

A Greek tragedy on a biblical theme may be considered Milton's final way of reconciling his Christianity with his humanism, and perhaps taken as evidence (assuming that *Samson* really was his last work, which cannot be proved) that Christ's repudiation of Greek literature in *Paradise Regained* does not mean Milton's own repudiation of his classical interests. At any rate, he takes up again the theme of temptation and the trials to which a good man could be subjected, but choosing as his hero this time not a perfect man, of whom there was only one example in history and who, as the Son of God, was in a very special position and so not entirely satisfactory as a symbol of man in the world, but a man guilty of human weaknesses. Samson had long been established in Christian tradition as a hero and a saint (though the primitive violence of the story in Judges made it a tricky business for patristic and other commentators to establish him as such), largely as a result of the reference to him in the eleventh chapter of the Epistle to the Hebrews as an example of those who triumphed through faith. And, as Professor Michael Krouse has shown in his *Milton's Samson and the Christian Tradition*, the story of Samson developed at the end of generations of mediaeval ecclesiastical and other writers as a tragedy in the mediaeval sense, an 'account of a great man, a saint, counterpart of Hercules, a type of Christ, who falls from happiness to misery'. And in non-ecclesiastical texts he appears as a great man who fell through weakness, his foolish love and trust of a bad woman. Renaissance poets developed the mediaeval view of Samson as a great man brought low by his trust of a faithless woman. His weakness, his *hamartia,* was lust or passion or imprudence or all three. The emphasis was on the latter part of Samson's career, and the stories in Judges of his earlier exploits were for the most part glossed over—as well they might be, for they are a very odd collection of acts of violence and brutality on all sides, which, though allegorized into edifying meanings by Church writers, were not easily amenable to serious literary treatment.

Milton's choice of Samson as a hero is not as arbitrary and as personal as has often been thought. Christian traditions about Samson available to Milton were strong and numerous. In Professor Krouse's words: 'During Milton's own lifetime Samson was remembered by many as a tragic lover; as a man of prodigious strength; as the ruler and liberator of Israel; as a great historical personage whose downfall was caused by the treachery of a woman, and therefore as an example of the perils of passion; as a sinner who repented and was restored to grace; as the original of Hercules; as a consecrated Nazarite; as a saint resplendent in unfailing faith; as an agent of God sustained by the Holy Spirit; and as a figure of Christ.' Milton, of course, brought to his treatment of the theme his own experience and his own interest in the temptations of the dedicated man and in the conflicting claims of public and private life. The result is an interesting blend of traditional and personal interpretations of the meaning of the last phase of Samson's life. Technically, too, Milton was inspired by the complex nature of Greek dramatic verse and by hints from the dramatic verse of such Italian poets as Tasso and Guarini to go beyond the relatively restricted scope of his epic blank verse, to develop in the choruses new kinds of poetic rhythms and to use variety of line-lengths and intermittent rhyme and suggestions of rhyme with a virtuosity unparalleled elsewhere in English poetry.

The tragedy is in the form of a series of dialogues between Samson and the various people who visit him, one at a time, with intervening monologues by Samson, comments by the Chorus, and the final reported account of Samson's death in pulling down the heathen temple on the Philistines. In the course of the action Samson gradually (and not always in a continuous forward movement) recovers a proper state of mind, which combines penitence, recognition of the nature of his earlier fault and of the justice of his present fate, and a confident submission to whatever destiny God has in store for him. The temptations which face him, a blind prisoner of the heathen Philistines, are despair on the one hand and a belief in his own ability to decide his destiny (instead of waiting on God's revelation of His purpose) on the other. In the end, God's purpose is revealed, and Samson goes to participate in the Philistine festival knowing that that is what God wishes him to do. His death in destroying his enemies was the destiny prepared for him.

The theme of the play is the process of Samson's recovery, and each of the characters who visit him—his father Manoah, his wife Dalila, the Philistine giant Harapha (an invention of Milton's), and the Philistine officer who comes to bid him to the festival—represent different temptations, in resisting which he proceeds further towards recovery and establishes his status as a hero. Only on some such reading of *Samson Agonistes* can full sense be made out of it, can all its features be reconciled and understood, and can Johnson's charge that it has a beginning and an end but no middle be refuted.

—David Daiches, *Milton* (London: Hutchinson University Library, 1957): pp. 230–32.

Ernest Sprott on Milton's Art of Prosody

[Ernest Sprott taught English Literature at McGill University.]

Samson Agonistes is metrically the pinnacle of its author's achievement. Like *Comus* it gathers up all his experience in previous works and carries it to a further stage of development. In its preface that principle of composition according to 'Stanza's or Pauses' which had ever been a guiding light for the poet receives articulate expression:

> The measure of Verse us'd in the Chorus is of all sorts, call'd by the Greeks *Monostrophic*, or rather *Apolelymenon*, without regard had to *Strophe, Antistrophe* or *Epod*, which were a kind of Stanza's fram'd only for the Music, then us'd with the Chorus that sung; not essential to the Poem, and therefore not material; or being divided into Stanza's or Pauses, they may be call'd *Allæostropha*.

Even when writing in Latin Milton had preferred this open form, and those critics who deal in parode and stasimon and epode and their like should beware that they do not go further than their author would go with them.

Little more need be said, except to comment on some of the more striking results of the emancipated verse.

Samson Agonistes contains in its lyrical portions, and there alone, twenty-seven Alexandrines. The six lines in pentameter context which may be Alexandrines are better elided to pentameters, for there are no certain examples of twelve syllable lines within the blank verse. But it should be noted that when Milton changes his prosody within a work he introduces the new scheme gradually, and even here in the lyric context some lines are doubtful hexameters. Midverse breaks appear in these later Alexandrines after all syllables from the fourth to the tenth, except the ninth, and in six lines there are two breaks; thus the lines become part of their essentially blank verse context, with the sense variously drawn into and out of them, and differ greatly from the early Alexandrines in The Hymn, 'On the Morning of Christs Nativity', where there are only three midverse breaks in twenty-eight examples.

Inversions in *Samson Agonistes* are much freer than anywhere else in Milton. This is not to be taken to mean that there are more inversions; surprisingly enough, the statistics reveal that there are if anything fewer. But in their combination in the line there is greater licence. There are, for instance, fifteen lines in which both first and second feet are inverted, and five of these are in the pentameter context.

The most drastic relaxation of principles occurs with the appearance of a new rule which permits monosyllabic feet. There are seventeen examples of this, all in the lyrical sections. It is difficult to say whether Milton would have regarded the lines as being trochaic with the last foot catalectic, or as iambic with the first foot catalectic. I take them as the latter to be consistent with my earlier treatment of the octosyllabics, and because of the occasional appearance of rhyme. If they are rightly to be thought of as trochaic, then here are seventeen cases in which there are three and four inversions to the line.

— Ernest S. Sprott, *Milton's Art of Prosody* (Oxford: Clarendon Press, 1958): pp. 131–32.

FRANK TEMPLETON PRINCE ON THE ITALIAN ELEMENT IN MILTON'S VERSE

[F. T. Prince was professor of English at Southampton University. He wrote several books of poetry, including *Soldiers Bathing*, and was the editor of the New Arden edition of *Shakespeare's Poems*.]

Yet there is one final observation to be made on the apparent freedom of the choruses in *Samson,* and that will lead to a deeper analysis of their structure. It is that, in spite of their almost wanton variety of rhythm and pattern, their freedom is of a solidified massive kind which corresponds to the freedom of Milton's blank verse: it is a legal, or even legalistic, freedom, which comes at times to seem no freedom at all, but a most ironic form of captivity. Everyone feels that the choruses in *Samson* disport themselves according to law, though few have been able to detect, or at least to formulate, the code which governs them. Their self-licensed liberty of movement is not, of course, to be distinguished entirely from the self-imposed artifice of their language. Any liberty which Milton sought would naturally be restricted by his notions of 'magnificence', of decorum, of using 'English words in a foreign idiom'. But the strangely limited liberty of these choruses may be related directly to their metrical basis, to their being, as the blank verse of *Paradise Lost* is, based upon Italian prosody.

That prosody is based upon rhyme, even when rhyme disappears, as in *versi sciolti,* or is used but sparingly, as in the semi-lyrical passages of the dramas. It has been suggested that traces of the influence of rhyme are to be found in the line-endings in Milton's blank verse, where we find that the tenth syllable is the pivot of the line and must be given a word such as would be either a good sonorous rhyme-word or capable of being given a certain stress. The same influence is seen at work in the choruses of *Samson Agonistes,* and demonstrates their kinship, not only to Milton's blank verse in general, but to the Italian originals of both.

The Italians may be said to have made the discovery that in a prosody based on rhyme one might write lyric verse which was lightly or only occasionally rhymed, provided that one retained or heightened the diction and movement of lyric poetry. Milton has but applied this discovery to English, dropping the Italian conventions of elision and allowing himself, as a substitute for these, a greater variety of line-lengths in his choral verse.

—Frank Templeton Prince, *The Italian Element in Milton's Verse* (Oxford: Oxford University Press, 1954): pp. 164–66.

A.S.P. Woodhouse on Tragic Effect in *Samson Agonistes*

[A.S.P. Woodhouse wrote extensively on English Renaissance authors. His critical works include *Milton the Poet* and *The Heavenly Muse: A Preface to Milton.*]

To say that *Samson Agonistes* is Milton's attempt to write a Christian tragedy is not to deny all relevance to his Greek models. It simply means that we must not expect divergent assumptions to issue in identical effects and must be willing to extend our terms of reference. Though many critics have followed Macaulay in asserting that Euripides is Milton's principal model, there seems to be singularly little ground for this opinion. In spirit his closest affinity is with Aeschylus, whose ethical and theological emphasis Milton can hardly have failed to appreciate, and who, in the *Oresteia*, re-reads an ancient and barbaric legend with all the insight of a profound moral and religious sensibility. In form, on the other hand, as Jebb recognizes (though his choice of the *Trachiniae* is not the happiest example) Sophocles is the chief mode; and this is confirmed by Parker, who rightly chooses the *Oedipus at Colonus* as the closest of all Greek analogues. But the similarity in form, and up to a point in content, serves to underline the difference in spirit and effect.

Though standing somewhat apart from Sophocles' other works, and modifying the inferences to be drawn from them, the *Oedipus at Colonus* is his deliberately chosen conclusion, which supplies the mitigation wholly lacking in the *Oedipus Tyrannus;* and it must be read in the light of the whole story and of the Sophoclean outlook. That outlook, if we follow H.D.F. Kitto, posits a cosmic order encompassing and governing the life of man. It is not a moral order such as Aeschylus presented as progressively realized; at most it subsumes such an order. Whoever runs athwart this cosmic order, whether wilfully or, like Oedipus, without intent, is (in Kitto's vivid image) like one who interrupts the flow of a powerful electric current, which destroys him and flows on. The gods have predicted, they have not decreed, the fate of Oedipus. Now he reaches Colonus, conscious that there he is to be released from suffering and the final prediction fulfilled. The prelude to this event is a series of encounters, much as in *Samson Agonistes.* The effect of these encounters is to magnify the figure of Oedipus from the blind and helpless wanderer of the opening scene to one of heroic proportions once more, with power to confer benefit and doom. In so far there is a parallel effect in Samson. But Oedipus' determination is not formed by these encounters: it is merely exhibited. Though (to steal a phrase from Dryden) it seems like treason in the court of Apollo to say it, the *Oedipus at Colonus* lies much more open to Johnson's charge than does *Samson Agonistes:* the action does not precipitate the catastrophe, as in Milton's tragedy it plainly does. Oedipus' reliance on divine prediction, and his determination to await its fulfilment at all hazards, had been already reached in the long interval since the ghastly revelations of the *Oedipus Tyrannus*, and especially in the year of wandering that had led at last to Colonus. Milton has chosen the much more difficult task of displaying in four acts a gradual change of mind in his hero comparable in extent to the whole development of Oedipus from the time when he stood before the palace blinded and desperate. The catastrophes, when at last they come, present some similarities: each hero goes to meet his end willingly and with a sense of fulfilment. But the effect in the two cases is very different. It must be so for dramatic reasons as well as philosophical—in the light, that is, not merely of the outlook of the two poets, but of the prior experiences of the two heroes. Oedipus has erred unwittingly: contemplating his deeds he has known an abyss of horror, but no remorse of conscience: his *hubris* perhaps supplied the trigger of the weapon that destroyed him, but certainly not the charge: and now he awaits release, as Samson has also dome. But Samson's experience has been of a different order: he has sinned, been punished, and repented, and he has been miraculously restored to God's service. The *Oedipus at Colonus* ends in mystery, and, partly because the known reality is so intolerable, mystery is relief. *Samson Agonistes* ends in the transcending of mystery, and in something that is more like triumph than mere relief: death is indeed relief—but death is swallowed up in victory. Both plays announce an end to weeping and lamentation; but to realize to the full the difference, one has only to place beside Milton's final chorus the final chorus of Sophocles (as it is movingly rendered by a recent translator):

> This is the end of tears:
> No more lament.
> Through all the years
> Immutable stands this event.

It would be hard to imagine any comment more noncommittal.

—A.S.P. Woodhouse, "Tragic Effect in *Samson Agonistes,*" *University of Toronto Quarterly* 28 (1958–59): pp. 205–22.

Roy Daniells on the Baroque Qualities of *Samson Agonistes*

[Roy Daniells was the head of the Department of English at the University of British Columbia. He has two volumes of poetry.]

The apparent simplicity of Milton's result is in fact a further proof of the dexterity of his technique. He achieves extreme concentration upon a single character and a single theme: Samson completely overshadows the remaining characters; he is always at the centre of our attention, even when absent from the stage. The episodes of the biblical story, moreover, are manipulated so as to provide unity of action; they are alluded to at various appropriate moments of the play and their materials distributed so that they cannot distract from the central theme—what is happening in Samson's heart and mind during the last hours of his life.

The new rationalism supplies another unifying agent. This Milton uses with a delicate touch, out of deference to his supernatural materials but there are clear signs of that new appreciation of reason which (whether in the Society of Jesus or in the Royal Society) was pervading seventeenth-century thought. The miraculous elements in Samson's story are not stressed; his feats of strength are made reasonable; his acts, however strange, are rationally accounted for. At the centre of the drama is Samson's will, and it is the part of reason to bring his will into alignment with the will of God.

Milton has realized with complete success that Baroque quality which critics refer to as tension of opposites, as ambiguity or paradox. Much of it comes easily out of the fundamental paradox of biblical material and classical form. Samson to the seventeenth-century reader is irresistibly reminiscent of Hercules, the strong man who coped with all enemies, even death, yet at the same time Samson is a type of Christ who by his own death destroyed our enemies. Samson is also a martyr, whose function it is to witness and to suffer, and simultaneously a divine avenger who invokes and brings down wrath upon his enemies. It has already been shown that he was regarded as a saint, from which category Milton was careful not to remove him. Yet he committed suicide, an abhorred crime. Within the structure of the classical drama Samson must function as the hero, with a "flaw" that leads to his tragic end. The lament for

Samson Agonistes is, as we have pointed out, both classical and Christian. And the philosophic conclusion is similarly ambivalent. The suggestion is never dispelled that the hero has been unjustly treated by Providence: he has endured—"Samson hath quit himself like Samson." At the same time we are told reassuringly "With God not parted from him as was feared/But favouring and assisting to the end." ...

Milton's capacity to achieve unity is supported by an inexhaustible series of devices. The natural unity of the Greek tragic form is dovetailed into the achieved unity of Samson's character. The complete dominance of the play by the relation between Samson's will and God's will is sustained where the wills become one "with God not parted from him as was feared." The simple strength of the Hebrew Samson becomes identified with God's uncontrollable intent.

The conventions of Greek tragedy bend a little, as we have seen, to conduce to this totality of effect. The Aristotelian "middle" seems inadequately developed. The character of Samson absorbs all the minor characters. The time represented is only a very few hours. The play is intended, Milton tells us, to be read, so we have no producer like Lawes in *Comus* to consider.

Samson Agonistes brings to mind as its most natural analogue in architecture, Bernini's S. Andrea al Quirinale, in considering which we must keep in mind the dual opening which Bernini habitually offers to the student of literature. He presents an idea, a *concetto,* and he expresses this in a formal architectural idiom which has its own grammar and syntax. It is not to be expected that Bernini will tell the story of the apostle Andrew but rather that he will seize the moment of martyrdom to which this faithful fisherman's life has brought him, the moment of metamorphosis between earth and heaven, a moment which reveals both past and future, and this the disposition of his architectural units will bring home to us by devices beyond the power of words.

—Roy Daniells, *Milton, Mannerism and Baroque* (Toronto: University of Toronto Press, 1963): pp. 215–17.

Works by
John Milton

A Maske Presented at Ludlow Castle, 1634 (Comus). 1637.

Epitaphium Damonis. c. 1640.

Animadversions on the Remonstrants Defence, against Smectymnuus. 1641.

Of Prelatical Episcopacy, and Whether It May Be Deduc'd from The Apostolical Times. 1641.

Of Reformation: Touching Church-Discipline in England, and the Causes that Hitherto Have Hindered It. 1641.

An Apology against a Pamphlet Called A Modest Confutation of the Animadversions upon the Remonstrant against Smectymnuus. 1642.

The Reason of Church-Government Urg'd against Prelaty. 1642.

The Doctrine and Discipline of Divorce. 1643.

Areopagitica: A Speech for the Liberty of Unlicenc'd Printing. 1644.

The Judgement of Martin Buber, concerning Divorce (translator). 1644.

Of Education. 1644.

Colasterion: A Reply to a Nameless Answer against The Doctrine and Discipline of Divorce. 1645.

Poems, Both English and Latin. 1645.

Tetrachordon: Expositions upon the Foure Chief Places in Scripture, 1645.

Eikonoklastes: In Answer to a Book Intitul'd Eikon Basilike. 1649.

The Tenure of Kings and Magistrates. 1649.

Pro Populo Anglicano Defensio. 1651.

Pro Populo Anglicano Defensio Secunda. 1654.

Pro Se Defensio contra Alexandrum Morum. 1655.

The Cabinet-Council. 1658.

Considerations Touching the Likeliest Means to Remove Hirelings out of the Church. 1659.

A Treatise of Civil Power in Ecclesiastical Causes. 1659.

Brief Notes upon a Late Sermon, Titl'd, The Fear of God and the King *by Matthew Griffith.* 1660.

The Readie & Easy Way to Establish a Free Commonwealth. 1660.

Paradise Lost. 1667, 1674.

Accedence Commenc't Grammar. 1669.

Paradise Regain'd; to Which Is Added Samson Agonistes. 1671.

Artis Logicae Plenior Institutio. 1672.

Of True Religion, Haeresie, Schism, Toleration, and What Best Means May Be Us'd against the Growth of Popery. 1673.

Poems, & c., upon Several Occasions. 1673.

A Declaration. 1674.

Epistolarum Familiarum Liber Unus. 1674.

Literae Pseudo-Senatus Anglicani. 1676.

Character of the Long Parliament. 1681.

A Brief History of Moscovia. 1682.

Republican-Letters. 1682.

Letters of State, from the Year 1649 till the Year 1659. 1694.

Poetical Works. Ed. Patrick Hume. 1695.

Works. 1697.

A Complete Collection of the Historical, Political, and Miscellaneous Works of John Milton (3 vols). Ed. John Toland. 1698.

Poetical Works (2 vols). 1707.

Original Letters and Papers of State Addressed to Oliver Cromwell. Ed. John Nickolls. 1743.

Prose Works (7 vols.). Ed. Charles Symmons. 1806.

De Doctrina Christiana Libri Duo. Ed. Charles Richard Sumner. 1825.

Poetical Works (3 vols.). Ed. John Mitford. 1832.

Works in Verse and Prose (8 vols.). Ed. John Mitford. 1851.

Poetical Works (2 vols.). Ed. George Gilfillan. 1853.

Poetical Works (3 vols.). Ed. David Masson. 1874.

A Common-place Book. Ed. A. J. Horwood. 1876.

Sonnets. Ed. Mark Pattison. 1883.

Poetical Works. Ed. H. C. Beeching. 1900.

Poetical Works. Ed. William Aldis Wright. 1903.

Poems (2 vols.). Ed. Herbert J. C. Grierson. 1925.

Works (18 vols.). Ed. Frank Allen Patterson et al. 1931–38.

Private Correspondence and Academic Exercises. Ed. and tr. Phyllis B. Tillyard and E. M. W. Tillyard, 1932.

Poetical Works (2 vols.). Ed. Helen Darbishire. 1952–55.

Complete Prose Works (8 vols.). Ed. Don M. Wolfe et al. 1953–82.

The Cambridge Milton. Ed. John Broadbent et al. 1972–.

The Macmillan Milton. Ed. C. A. Patrides et al. 1972–.

Works about
John Milton

Abrams, M. H. *Five Types of Lycidas* in *Milton's Lycidas: The Tradition and the Poem*, ed. C. A. Pattrides. New York: Holt, Rinehart and Winston, 1961.

Adams, Richard P. "The Archetypal Pattern of Death in Milton's *Lycidas*." *PMLA* 64 (1949): 183–88.

Adams, Robert M. *Ikon: John Milton and the Modern Critics*. Ithaca: Cornell University Press, 1955.

Allen, D.C. *The Harmonious Vision: Studies in Milton's Poetry*. Baltimore: John Hopkins University Press, 1953.

Arthos, John. *Dante, Michelangelo and Milton*. New York: Humanities Press, 1963.

Banks, Theodore H., Jr. *Milton's Imagery*. New York: Columbia University Press, 1956.

Bloom, Harold. *A Map of Misreading*. New York: Oxford University Press, 1975.

Bridges, Robert. *Milton's Prosody*. Oxford: Clarendon Press, 1921.

Brisman, Leslie. *Milton's Poetry of Choice and Its Romantic Heirs*. Ithaca: Cornell University Press, 1973.

Brooks, Cleanth. "The Light Symbolism in 'L'Allegro—Il Penseroso.'" In *The Well Wrought Urn*. New York: Harcourt Brace Jovanovich, 1975.

Brooks, Cleanth, and Hardy, John Edward, eds. *Poems of Mr. John Milton: The 1642 Edition, with Essays in Analysis*. New York: Harcourt, Brace, 1952.

Cox, Lee Sheridan. "The 'Ev'ning Dragon' in *Samson Agonistes*: A Reappraisal." *Modern Language Notes* 76 (1961) 577–84.

Daiches, David. *Milton*. London: Hutchinson University Library, 1957.

Daniells, Roy. *Milton, Mannerism and Baroque*. Toronto: University of Toronto Press, 1963.

Empson, William. *Some Versions of Pastoral*. New York: New Directions, 1950.

————. *Milton's God*. London: Chatto and Windus, 1965.

Frye, Northrop. "Literature as Context: Milton's *Lycidas*." In *Fables of Identity: Studies in Poetic Mythology*. New York: Harcourt, Brace and World, 1963.

——————. *The Return of Eden: Five Essays on Milton's Epics*. Toronto: University of Toronto Press, 1965.

Goodman, Paul. "Milton's 'On His Blindness': Stanzas, Motion of Thought." In *The Structure of Literature*. Chicago: University of Chicago Press, 1954.

Goosman, Ann. "Milton's Samson as the Tragic Hero Purified by Trial." *Journal of English and Germanic Philology* 61 (1962): 528–41.

Hyman, Lawrence. "Milton's 'On the Late Massacre in Piedmon." *ELN*, 3 (1965):26–29.

Hollander, John. *The Untuning of the Sky: Ideas of Music in English Poetry 1500-1700*. Princeton: Princeton University Press, 1961.

——————. *The Figure of Echo: A Mode of Allusion in Milton and After*. Berkeley: University of California Press, 1981.

Kendall, Lyle. "Sonnet XIX and Wither's Emblem III.xlvii." *Studies in Philology*, 49 (1972): 57.

Kermode, Frank. "Milton's Hero." *Review of English Studies* 4 (1953): 317–30.

——————, ed. *The Living Milton*. London: Routledge and Keagan Paul, 1960.

Knott, John Ray. *Milton's Pastoral Vision*. Chicago: Chicago University Press, 1971.

Krouse, Michael. *Milton's Samson and the Christian Tradition*. Princeton: Princeton University Press, 1949.

Leishman, J.B. *Milton's Minor Poems*. London: Hutchinson, 1969.

Lewalski, Barbara Kieffer. "*Samson Agonistes* and the 'Tragedy' of the Apocalypse." *PMLA* 85 (1970): 1050–62.

Martz, Louis. *The Poet of Exile: A Study of Milton's Poetry*. New Haven: Yale University Press, 1980.

——————, ed. *Milton: A Collection of Critical Essays*. Englewood Cliffs, N.J.: Prentice Hall, 1966.

Patrides, C.A. *Milton and the Christian Tradition*. Oxford: Oxford University Press, 1966.

————, ed. *Milton's Lycidas: The Tradition and the Poem*. Columbia: University of Missouri Press, 1983.

Pequigney, Joseph. "Milton's Sonnet XIX Reconsidered." *TSLL* 8 (1967): 485–98.

Prince, Frank Templeton. *The Italian Element in Milton's Verse*. Oxford: Oxford University Press, 1954.

Ransom, John Crowe. "A Poem Nearly Anonymous." In *The World's Body*. New York: Charles Scribners' Sons, 1938.

Shumaker, Wayne. " 'Flowerets and Sounding Seas': A Study in the Affective Structure of *Lycidas*." *PMLA* 66 (1951): 485–494.

Spitzer, Leo. "Understanding Milton" in *Essays on English and American Literature*. Princeton: Princeton University Press, 1962.

Sprott, Ernest S. *Milton's Art of Prosody*. Oxford: Clarendon Press, 1958.

Stoehr, T. "Syntax and Poetic Form in Milton's Sonnets." *English Studies* 45 (1964): 289–301.

Stone, C.F. "Milton's Self-Concerns and Manuscript Revision in *Lycidas*." *Modern Language Notes* 83 (1968): 867–81.

Stroup, Thomas. "'When I Consider': Milton's Sonnet XIX." *Studies in Philology*, 69 (1972): 242–58.

Tuve, Rosemond. *Images and Themes in Five Poems by Milton*. Cambridge: Harvard University Press, 1957.

————. "Baroque and Mannerist Milton." *Journal of English and Germanic Philology* 60 (1961): 817–33.

Wheeler, Thomas. "Milton's Twenty-Third Sonnet." *Studies in Philology* 58 (1961): 510–15.

Wilkenfield, Roger B. "Act and Emblem: The Conclusion of *Samson Agonistes*." *English Literary History* 32 (1965): 160–68.

Woodhouse, A.S.P. "Tragic Effect in *Samson Agonistes*." *University of Toronto Quarterly* 28 (1958-9): 205–22.

Index of Themes and Ideas